HOW TO
PHOTOGRAPH WOMEN

HOW TO PHOTOGRAPH WOMEN

by Peter Gowland

Revised Edition

General Editor: Aaron Sussman

CROWN PUBLISHERS, Inc.

NEW YORK

Books by PETER GOWLAND

How to Photograph Women
Stereo Photography
Figure Photography
How to Take Glamour Photos
How to Take Better Home Movies
Glamour Techniques
Face and Figure
Glamour Camera
Photo Secrets
Electronic Flash Guide
Photo Ideas
The Figure
Camera in Hawaii
Camera in the Orient

Copyright, © 1954, 1967, by Crown Publishers, Inc.
Library of Congress Catalog Card Number: 54-11183
Printed in the United States of America

CONTENTS

To my wife, Alice, and my friend
Frank Fenner

Foreword

IT is hard to believe that the first edition of this book appeared a baker's dozen years ago!

It apparently satisfied a great need, and did it so well that it has remained in print, for most of the time in two editions, all of these years.

This speaks well for Peter Gowland, who has become in the interim the accredited specialist in the difficult but pleasant art of photographing women. Certainly no one else has produced a guidebook on the subject that has been so helpful, that has taught all of its secrets so freely and so clearly. No wonder it became, and has remained, an intercontinental *best* seller . . . a perdurable classic in its field.

And now Peter, with the help of his lovely wife, Alice, has completely revised and enlarged the text, bringing it up to date both technically and artistically. In addition, he has supplied almost a hundred new photographs to prove that his skill has never lost its hand, and that women are as much fun to photograph as they have ever been.

This new, revised edition of How to Photograph Women should appeal to photographers, artists, and anyone who likes to look at pictures. If you're a man, this book will tell you how to get the most out of your camera; if you're a woman, it will tell you what you need to know to become *photogenic* as well as *good to look at*. Though the two are not always synonymous, Peter Gowland has learned how to bring the two together. Here he tells how *he* does it and, inferentially, how *you* can do it.

Aaron Sussman

7

One of my favorite models—Diane Webber.

Chapter I

WHAT CAMERA DO YOU NEED?

DON'T worry about what camera to use. You can get good pictures with almost any camera—yes, even a box camera—provided, of course, there are pictures to take. Actually, the camera should be determined by the type of photographing you plan to do. No ONE camera with ONE lens will handle every type. With small cameras, you have economy and speed of operation, candidness, spontaneity; with a large camera you'll get slightly better quality and finer grain, but a slower and more awkward operation. The best camera for you probably is the one you are already used to.

The majority of magazine photography is done with 35mm and $2\frac{1}{4} \times 2\frac{1}{4}$. For my own work I use three cameras: a 35mm Pentax, a $2\frac{1}{4} \times 2\frac{1}{4}$ Hasselblad, and the 4x5 Gowlandflex. All of these cameras have one thing in common: Because they are reflex cameras you can see the full-size image on the ground glass and they all have interchangeable lenses.

9

Because I am a professional and am working for a variety of markets, I find it necessary to use larger film on specific occasions, such as when shooting calendars or covers. However, if the operation of the camera you now use has become automatic to you and, from a technical view, you are satisfied with its results, there is no point in changing.

If you don't have a camera, and are not familiar with the advantages and disadvantages of the different sizes, you might consider these points:

A Camera with Interchangeable Lenses

Most inexpensive cameras come with a standard focal-length lens (equal to the diagonal measurement of the film . . . 35mm requires a 2″ lens, $2\frac{1}{4}$x$2\frac{1}{4}$ a 3″ lens, 4x5 a 6″ lens) which gives you a fixed angle of view. On cameras with interchangeable lenses, it is possible to get anything from an extreme wide angle, such as you need when photographing a room, to a telephoto close-up of a distant object. These lenses will generally be required only for a small percentage of pictures, but they are nice to have. It's possible to purchase such a camera with only one lens and then add other lenses as you need them.

When photographing women, you may have occasion to shoot close-ups or portraits. With a standard focal-length lens you cannot get a large image on the negative without moving the camera close to the subject. And when you do that, unflattering distortion results. That is because the nose is too close to the camera and becomes disproportionately enlarged. The ears, being farther back, become smaller. If you get too close, the ears may even disappear altogether. Of course, you can stay back and enlarge the center of the film when printing, but then much negative space is wasted, and sharpness as well as fine grain is sacrificed.

Ground Glass vs. the Viewfinder

There are advantages favoring both the ground-glass and the range-finder types of cameras. The range-finder camera is best suited to news and fast sporting events where normal focal-length lenses are required. Since our stress is on glamour work, where the full use of the negative is desirable, and various focal-length lenses are used, the reflex camera is recommended. Either a single-lens camera or a twin lens is suitable.

In the smaller cameras, such as the 35mm, the reflex mirrors are small and the cameras are of sophisticated design so that it is possible

These two illustrations show how a short focal-length lens, if used too close to the subject, can cause distortion. The entire front part of the face seems to bulge toward the camera, while with a longer focal-length lens (right), features are proportioned naturally. A good thing to remember when buying a lens for portraits is to get one that is twice the diameter of the film.

to look through the lens, press the shutter, and have the mirror move up, the lens stop down, and the shutter fire. In the larger cameras, such as 4x5 format, all these operations are not as easily executed. The twin-lens design is more practical in the larger-size format because the viewing lens is always wide open and the mirror is stationary, thus eliminating vibration if it were to move. The lower lens is ready to record on the film what the upper lens sees.

Because my training was mainly with a reflex camera in the $2\frac{1}{4}$ size, I felt a sense of frustration having to work with a view camera when the larger film size was called for. This is one of the reasons I designed the Gowlandflex with twin lens and 4x5 format. This lightweight metal camera takes 4x5, 90mm, 70mm, and $2\frac{1}{4}$ film sizes. It is available with 180mm, 210mm, 240mm, and 360mm lenses. The body weighs less than 5 pounds, is 5" wide, and can be used easily for hand-held pictures outdoors and in the studio as well as on a tripod. It can be viewed from the top with hood and magnifying glass or from the back, eye level with reflex hood.

11

The single-lens reflex can change lenses, but there is the problem of seeing through the lens when it is stopped down; some are equipped with an automatic spring that stops the diaphragm down to a predetermined place when the shutter release is pressed. However, there is another disadvantage of the single-lens reflex camera: flash synchronization with the focal plane shutter is not practical in most cases. This is because the shutter, instead of being between the lens elements, is at the back of the camera, next to the film. You may have noticed it

A reflex camera is good for shooting pictures at the beach, park, or wherever you happen to take your model. Here I'm using my Hasselblad with Diane Schaeffer.

in the Graflex, for example; it is a rolled curtain with varying sized slits which travels across the film at different speeds, according to the exposure you wish. To synchronize flash with large bulbs, only the fastest speeds are practical. This means that in shooting color you are forced to use the lens almost wide open, which gives you a limited depth of field.

Since most strobes fire at over 1/1000th of a second, it is impossible to have the flash cover the full negative with the focal plane shutter of the Graflex, and it can be done only at 1/25th second on the Leica. This is impractical for outdoor shooting if you are using sunlight as your main light source.

Automatic Film Wind

An important feature to look for in a roll film camera is the automatic film wind. This is a built-in device for preventing double ex-

12

posures. You can't advance the film until a picture is taken and you can't snap another picture unless you recock the shutter by advancing the film. This leaves the photographer free to concentrate on the picture, instead of worrying about the mechanics of the camera. Most of the better roll film cameras have this feature.

Roll Film vs. Cut Film

Your choice of camera determines whether you use roll or cut film, since most of the small cameras use roll film and the larger cameras use cut film. There are advantages and disadvantages to both. From the standpoint of economy, roll film is quite a saving. With the 120 film, cost per negative is a little over six cents. Besides, roll film can be a time saver because there is no darkroom loading before a shooting session. You are never limited to the number of holders you have with you because there are no holders to bother about! Roll film is a time

saver in the darkroom, too. Six rolls or more can be developed in a deep Nikor tank in the same amount of time spent developing a dozen cut films. Time is also saved in drying, washing, and proofing. The greatest advantage in roll film is the vast selection of poses and expressions this low-cost medium affords. If you are not satisfied with a girl's expression or pose, four or five negatives of slightly different arrangement or angle can assure you that you have the best picture possible without worry about cost or extra work in the darkroom. Whenever roll film will do the job, I use it.

The main advantage to cut film is in commercial work and in portraiture. The large-size film is easier to retouch, and the finished picture does not exaggerate the retouching strokes as happens so often on the small films. Many times, when shooting commercial pictures of lingerie or sportswear, it may be necessary to use retouching so that the items appear flawless on the finished picture. When small negatives are used, it is advisable to air-brush the finished print rather than try to retouch the negative.

14

WHAT CAMERA DO YOU NEED?

The amateur who is shooting pictures for his own pleasure can very well get by with one camera. The professional can get by with two (a roll film camera and a sheet film camera).

If a photographer does add another camera to his collection, it need not cost a fortune. When I was getting started and had only a roll film miniature, I wanted to do portraits of professional quality. I bought a 4x5 view camera for twenty dollars and a ten-inch rapid rectilinear lens for seven dollars. It was the best portrait lens I ever had. All my best portraits have been made with that lens.

My 4x5 Gowlandflex enables me to shoot color in the ocean without a tripod.

Most calendar markets prefer 4x5 or larger film so I generally carry my twin-lens Gowlandflex on location.

16

Chapter II

SHOULD YOU DEVELOP YOUR OWN?

HAVE you been developing your films, or do you send them to the corner drugstore for processing? Don't laugh at the words "corner drugstore," because that's the natural place for the beginner or amateur to go. It's fine, too, provided you've made sure that the lab which does their work is competent.

The average snapshot shooter doesn't really know the difference between a good and bad print. Photography itself is such a miracle to him that *any* image, fuzzy or sharp, is wonderful. But to those of you who want to get the best possible results from your camera, the lab work is important. It isn't necessary, however, to do your own developing and printing in order to get perfect results. Almost every city has a photographic lab that caters to the professional and serious amateur. I sent most of my work to such a lab until I was able to buy the equipment to do it myself. Their results were excellent. I was sure of consistent negatives, and the pick-up and delivery service was an added convenience. Prices vary. I've had such service for as low as fifty cents a roll. Once you've established an account with a professional lab, they will cooperate in giving added services such as printing your name on your pictures, putting the negatives in individual glassine envelopes, etc.

Leave Everything Spick-and-Span

If you don't have a darkroom, and your wife or mother or landlady is sympathetic to your photographic ambitions, perhaps you can use either the kitchen or the bathroom. One way to assure their cooperation is by leaving it just as spick-and-span as you find it. Even more so, if you have the energy. I've seen professional darkrooms that look as though they were shot out of a gun . . . and usually the photog-

17

rapher is a nervous wreck from looking for lost negs, etc. Start out with the idea of a place for everything and everything in its place, and your photography will be more fun.

There is, on the market now, a portable darkroom. It's a box on wheels, partitioned to hold enlarger, trays, paper, chemicals, etc. Wheeling it into the kitchen or bathroom when you're ready to process is easy. The top is used as your printing table. I should imagine that anyone with a slight knowledge of woodwork could build one like it inexpensively.

But whether you use a makeshift or permanent darkroom, the success of your lab work will depend largely on how well you understand the capacities of your film and developer.

The Developer

There are many different brands on the market. By testing you can find the one that suits you best. Fine-grain developers are best for roll film or small-size cut film. Use the replenisher method in developing and add replenisher as needed to keep the gallon level. When I have used a gallon of replenisher and a gallon of developer, I discard the mixture and begin with a new gallon of D-76. This developer is an old standard, considered by many photographers to be not as fine grain

I develop six rolls of 120 film at a time, using Nikor reels and tank. The tank cost $10.00 and the reels around $3.50 each.

18

By making a series of tests at various f stops using one speed, you will be able to determine the correct exposure for your particular equipment. In this instance I used 1/500th at f/2.8 to 1/500th at f/22. I was able to judge which exposure was the best.

as more exotic expensive formulas, but I have found it to be very stable and consistent over a period of time, while some of the other developers have decreased considerably in strength as they were stored and used.

Test As You Go

Forgive me if I seem to stress testing, but I'm a firm believer in the saying "One test is worth a thousand expert opinions." Whenever

19

you are in doubt about a new kind of film, or the light output of a flash, make several negatives at different exposures and develop them for the normal time. Pick the exposure that suits you and you have the correct film or flash speed.

To test developers, try a brand recommended by professionals. One way to know what professionals use is to study the photo data listed with photographic credits. When you've found the one that produces satisfactory results, stick to it and to the exposure arrived at through testing. Thus you standardize a portion of your operation and eliminate guesswork.

Even if you are having your negatives developed by a lab, testing is a good practice. Especially so because some labs are inclined to use their developer for months, until it becomes so weak that an extra stop or two is required to produce a normal negative. But don't let this worry you because a better negative for extreme enlargements is made by overexposure and underdevelopment.

Stick to One Film

I hate to recommend a certain film and say it is better than any other. I don't know what is best. I haven't tried them all. But I have found two films that work for my kind of pictures—Adox 17 and Eastman Tri-X. An asa of 40 is used with Adox and the Tri-X is asa 400. I use the Tri-X only when a fast film is called for. I feel more confident when using these same films for all of my black-and-white pictures.

I usually shoot my outdoor pictures when the sun is shining or at least when there is a haze. When I am working indoors, I use floods, spots, or strobe, so I don't have to go to the extremes in film speed and "hot souping."

The Enlarger

Your choice of enlarger will be based entirely on your needs and your financial status. It isn't necessary to buy the most expensive. My 5x7 enlarger cost twenty-five dollars new, and I've had over ten years of good use out of it.

Just as I advise simplified shooting and developing, so do I suggest that your printing be more or less standardized, too. If you familiarize yourself with one brand of paper, know its speed and characteristics, your printing operations will be accurate and quicker. And you'll have less waste.

Lately I have been using an enlarging meter to speed up my printing. It saves the work of making test strips and gives an accurate time and exposure to use. The meter is placed on the enlarging easel so that the model's face is projected on the white disk. The enlarger is then stopped down until the cross, or spot, on the meter, disappears. The meter can be set on any number of seconds desired and the only thing that varies with each negative is the lens opening.

Three tips to remember: For fine-grain negatives, slightly overexpose the negative, and underdevelop. For more contrast (when pictures are taken with flat light) underexpose and overdevelop. When making large prints (16x20) use paper one grade harder.

Darkrooms

For those of you who are thinking of building a darkroom, here is a word of encouragement. You don't need a large lab even for professional work. The smaller the room, the less walking you will have to do. I remember the first darkroom I had (after the developing in the bathroom and kitchen stage). It was a converted bedroom, about 12'x 12', and every time I made a print I had to walk across the room and back, twenty-four feet! After a few enlargements I was ready to lie down.

I have two darkrooms now. Each is 7'x7'. In one I do all the film loading, developing, drying, and I also use it for copying pictures (Fig. 1). In the other I do the printing (Fig. 2). Each room has a worktable on one side and a sink on the other so I can make a print and turn to develop it without getting up from my stool.

I built the sinks and worktables for both darkrooms myself. Both are made with 3/4″ plywood. There is no metal used in the sinks (7'x30″ x35″ high), and they don't leak! The secret is in slanting the bottom from each end to a center drain (the same principle as a steep roof; the more the slant, the less likely it is to leak). The difference between the two sinks is that in the film room I made the center drain lower by about a foot so that I could lower the 22″ Nikor tanks into this slot and thus the top of the tanks would be the same height as the 1-gallon color-processing tanks—much easier to work with in loading, rinsing, and so on. I didn't put racks or drawers beneath the sinks in either room but use the space for various storage materials that change from time to time.

Above the sinks are storage shelves for paper, film holders, chemicals, and various miscellaneous items.

I have attached 30 clothespins (15 on each side) to a bracket that pulls down from the drying cupboard. This holds the strips of film while they are drying. When the film is attached the bracket is pushed up into place, the door is closed, and the 500-watt heating element in a tube goes to work.

Between these two darkrooms is a small finishing room. I built a counter that incorporates a viewing box on top and use this to make a

22

black-and-white negative copy of color transparencies that are sent out (Fig. 5). This same counter is used to do all the stamping, weighing, and mailing. Above are storage shelves for mailers, brochures, and so on (Fig. 6). Below are drawers and a space for my various camera cases, most of them loaded and ready to go.

I have eliminated the record player that I had in my previous darkroom, but because I still enjoy music, I do have a radio and a speaker that is connected to a high-fi set. One trouble with this is that occasionally my teen-age daughter puts on one of her records when I'm in the darkroom and practically blasts me off the stool!

5

6

Chapter III

YOU AND THE MODEL

"WHERE do you find your models?" is the first question most beginners ask me. It's their common belief that professional photographers hire their models through agencies, and the mere thought of talking with a businesslike secretary who throws such frightening questions as "What are the pictures for?" and "How many hours will you guarantee?" topped by the final blow of "Our girls get $25.00 an hour," is enough to scare any photographic ambitions out of them. I know. After my first contact with an agency, I wanted to turn my camera in.

But my common sense told me that there must be pretty girls who aren't connected with an agency: girls who are still in school, or others who never thought of themselves as being pretty enough to register with a model agency.

Where to Find Models

One of my best and most popular cover girls was working as a waitress when a friend of mine saw her. He knew I was looking for

25

models, so he gave her my card, and a few days later she called on me. Another model, who became tops in the fashion field, we discovered at a benefit dance. Our latest, a gorgeous green-eyed blonde with a figure second to none, was working as a dental assistant.

There are all kinds of ways to discover new faces. Newspapers are always running pictures of pretty young girls as "Miss Something-or-other." Television is another medium to bring them to your attention.

I was walking through a hardware store not too long ago when I noticed an attractive blonde girl selling cookies in front of the store. She had a beautiful face with a bright, even smile, and when she asked if I would buy some cookies to help her school, I obliged. This gave me an opportunity to give her my card. I was careful not to ask for her telephone number but instead told her she was welcome to bring her parents with her, if she cared to be interviewed as a model. A week later she and her parents came to the studio and when they found that I was a legitimate photographer, they were happy to have her work for me.

It's difficult to approach girls on the street, but if you make your speech brief and to the point, friendly but not personal, and carry cards wih your name, telephone number, and address, which you can give them (making plain the invitation to bring along a friend or relative), they'll have no cause to be offended.

In your own immediate circle of friends there may be a girl who would love to model and is just waiting to be asked. If you keep your eyes open for beauty you'll have a good chance of increasing your list of models.

The Question of $

How you pay your model, and what you pay her, depends on what you are going to do with the pictures. If you are an amateur and ask a girl to pose so that you can have pictures for your own pleasure, she should be happy to accept prints in payment for her time. If the model you use is a professional, she may want to be paid but will not charge as much since you are not going to sell the pictures. If you are a beginner and wish to try your luck at selling your work, yet are not sure if it will sell, ask your model if she will work for you on a percentage basis. She gets paid when the pictures sell. A fair amount would be ten per cent or fifteen per cent or fifty per cent, depending on how much you like the model.

If you are a professional photographer, I think you will agree it is better to pay the model whether she is a professional or not. Making

Test shots.

extra prints can be a time waster, and percentages are a bother to keep track of, especially if you do a volume of work.

Take Some Test Shots First

Before I invest in a model fee or in a great quantity of materials, I take a series of test shots. These are usually only on $2\frac{1}{4} \times 2\frac{1}{4}$ film and are of the model's face, figure, or both, depending on what type of model she is. I would much rather judge a girl by my own pictures than by the ones she shows me. We all know what retouching can do, as well as how appearances can change in a few months, so I advise a few minutes and a few negatives first. If you're quick, and don't take too much of the girl's time, she usually is very willing to oblige.

The Model Release

Once you've taken pictures of a girl, no matter for what purpose, it's advisable to obtain a model release. Nothing long and involved. Just a simple statement giving her consent for you to use the pictures should you, at some future date, have an opportunity to sell one or two. If she is a minor, her parents will have to sign the release also. Here is a copy of the release I use for all sittings:

PETER GOWLAND
609 Hightree Road
Santa Monica, California
GL 4-7867

Date _____

In consideration of _____, paid me by Peter Gowland, receipt of which is hereby acknowledged, I, _____, consent that you, your customers, agents and assigns, may use my name, portraits or pictures, for advertising or commercial purposes or for the purposes of trade.

_____ L.S.

Address _____

As parents or guardian of the above-named person, I consent to the above release and signature thereto and to the uses therein set forth.

_____

Address _____

I had several hundred printed up for a very small sum and they've saved time wasted in tracking down a girl whose pictures didn't sell until a year or so after being taken. It's best to have the release signed the day you shoot the pictures.

Keep the Model Happy

More important to the finished pictures than any of the preceding suggestions is your attitude toward the model when you are working. A prime requisite—be happy! Your pictures will be a reflection not only of the way a girl looks but also of how she feels. Unless your model enjoys the time she spends before the camera your pictures are apt to reflect a mood of boredom.

One of the first questions I ask a girl before we leave for location is, "Have you eaten?" If you want a vivacious model, full of pep and enthusiasm, keep her well fed. I always carry a bag of fruit and several bottles of pop just in case she shows signs of weakening. I never work

30

too long at a time, either. Pause for a break, now and then, and the work will seem more like fun.

Never try to "talk a girl into modeling." If she doesn't show interest in posing, you'll be wise to forget her. There's nothing worse than wasting your time on a yawning, sighing individual who would much rather be some place else.

And Don't Get Personal

Whether you're a professional or an amateur, keep your photography on an impersonal basis. Don't be a wise guy. Keep your hands on your camera. When you pose her, direct her, don't push. Never use your photography as a means of making dates or getting a girl out in the woods.

Keep Promises

If you promise her pictures, keep your promise. After all, your model works as hard as you do—if not harder—and pictures can often help her in getting other jobs.

So, whether you use your sister, your girlfriend, the theatre cashier, a waitress, or a professional model, your results depend on your own attitude and your judgment in selecting a subject. If you gain the confidence and respect of one girl, she'll readily act as press agent in telling her friends about you. The more people you have looking for models, the higher the percentage of really attractive girls you'll have to select from.

Proof Sheet

All my 120 pictures are proofed in strips of four, three strips to a sheet of 8x10 enlarging paper. The negatives and paper are placed in an 8x10 printing frame and the light from the enlarger is used to expose the paper. Most prints with normal negatives run five seconds with the enlarger lens stopped down to $f/8$. I prefer this method to contact printing because (1) I need to buy only one paper for enlarging or contact printing, (2) the same filters can be used for both contact and enlarging with Varigam paper, (3) I can dodge while printing, should there be variations in exposure between the twelve negatives.

Since there was a $\frac{1}{2}''$ space unused at the side of the sheet, I had a litho negative with my name and address made. Now there is no waste; and when my proof sheets go to the publishers, stamping is un-

necessary. On most stories, I generally number each 120 negative with India ink. Some stories run 200 to 300 negatives. On a dance series, the model and I often make 150 shots in a couple of hours. By using the number system, the editor can phone or wire the numbers he wants enlarged, thus saving a couple of days for mail to reach Los Angeles from New York. Model fees and other costs being what they are, I feel that film is the cheapest part of the job, so I do not try to save on that. The more pictures taken, the better the selection of poses to choose from.

The negatives are cut in strips of four and they are filed in glassine envelopes made to take strips that size. I find that the longer strips are easier to handle, and can be more easily reproofed.

The contact sheet shown here was made of a prospective model, Sally Carter, who came to the studio for an interview. When we find a

32

model we think will work out well for us, Mrs. Gowland has her try on a costume suitable to her type, and I then shoot a roll with the Hasselblad. I almost always give the girl contacts or enlargements for her trouble. By taking at least twelve pictures in various poses and angles, I can then decide what to do and what not to do the day we work together. That's how I discover her good angles.

The best picture from the test shots is glued to a 3"x5" card with the model's address, age, height, weight, measurements of bust, waist and hips, color of eyes, hair and length, experience, hobbies and birthplace—the latter two in case we wish to write a little blurb about the girl later. We feel that this filing system takes a little time, but how can a photographer remember beautiful models without a picture?

Close-compact poses can look as candid and appealing as full-lengths, even though each portion of the body has been posed beforehand.

Chapter IV

DRESS AND UNDRESS

THAT old adage "Clothes make the man" applies more to photography than to everyday life. Whether your model is your sweetheart, your sister, your wife, or just a friend, the clothes she wears will largely affect the professional quality of your finished picture. It isn't necessary for the photographer to be a connoisseur of the latest fashions, but it is important that he recognize the different types of models in order to determine which clothes category they fit best.

The Four Categories

Basically there are four classifications: *junior miss, glamour girl, bathing beauty,* and *fashion.* Every model fits into one or the other of these. Sometimes, more than one. The average girl doesn't always place herself in the correct category, so it's up to you, as the photographer, to analyze your subject and decide which type she fits best. Women, as a rule, like to think of themselves as the glamour type. This can be very trying for the photographer who has not learned how, tactfully, to make their correct category more appealing.

The very young girl, with slight build, long legs, but not too curvaceous, is definitely the junior miss. Shorts and sweater, bathing suits, sportswear are her best costumes. These are standard apparel for the average teen-ager, so you should have no trouble in obtaining them. However, make sure the shorts and bathing suit are conservative; with the junior miss, sex appeal is not the main theme.

The glamour girl, on the other hand, should have a beautiful face, long soft hair, curvaceous figure. Lacy blouses or negligees, low-cut evening gowns, feminine and revealing dresses are perfect apparel for emphasizing her sexy qualities.

The bathing beauty is the girl with a combination of well-proportioned figure and pretty face. She can pose in brief shorts and form-

The junior miss poses well in bathing suit. Shorty nightgowns and photographic lingerie are available at reasonable prices—photographers should keep several on hand.

fitting swim suits. Although she has sex appeal, hers is the outdoor, vivacious variety.

The fashion model is the girl with a very slim figure. Her hair is usually in high style and according to the latest fad, which could be anything from extremely short to bouffant with curls. In the last few years fashion editors have given their pictures a more sexy slant. I've made some very nice glamour shots with fashion models, but it isn't always easy to find a girl who will do any kind of bare or seminude poses if she is active in the fashion world. When you do, the result is something more classy than the ordinary pin-up.

What About the Clothes?

Now that we've briefed the needs of each classification, your next question will probably be: "Where do I get the clothes?" It's a good question. Even professional photographers have to be constantly on the lookout for new and interesting photographic costumes. They have an advantage over the amateur in that the client usually pays for such items, but they still have to shop around before they find just what they want. For the amateur, or beginner, the girl's own wardrobe will be

38

sufficient. Since each model fits into only one or two groups, you need not worry about the clothes you want to photograph her in. Just let her know in advance what you want her to wear; if she doesn't have these, she can undoubtedly borrow them from a friend or relative.

Plain Colors Best

In every type of costume, plain colors rather than prints are preferred. There are exceptions to this, however, with the advent of pop art and the many interesting designs in women's fabrics, when for variety some really "far out" glamour can be created. In bathing suits, or brief costumes used for calendar or advertising, the pictures are more acceptable when the colors are plain. When using color film it is easier to get away with a patterned fabric because the colors themselves

Barbara Boucher (left) wears bathing suit designed and made by model, Barbara Osterman. Teri Reno (right) is typical of the junior-type model.

Sometimes a length of chiffon material can be used to simulate a negligee for interior settings.

separate; however, when using black-and-white film the effect would be a conglomeration of varying shades of grays. The junior miss is about the only one who can get away with flowered or patterned swimsuits. Her pictures should feature whimsical poses exemplifying youth, rather than the curvaceous, provocative attitude of the pin-up. As a rule, the junior miss gives the least amount of trouble as far as wardrobe is concerned.

The Specialized Wardrobe

The glamour girl, on the other hand, requires a more specialized wardrobe. Not all girls possess a filmy negligee, or a décolleté evening gown; but usually, if they make an effort, they can borrow one, or even buy an inexpensive one that will serve for pictures. One short cut I've found in photographing head and shoulder shots is to have someone make up just the top of an evening dress or negligee. Any dressmaker would be happy to do this for a small fee, and it would be worth your while to have a collection of such items for future use. Maybe your model has some sewing talent. Find out. She will, no doubt, be willing to make up anything you suggest, especially if she knows it's to her advantage.

A yard or two of alluring fabrics, such as velvet, satin, lace, silver or gold lamé, can be utilized on head-and-shoulder portraits just by wrapping it around the model to simulate a strapless evening dress. It doesn't take more than a yard or two to serve as a background on close-ups. Sometimes it's just what the picture needs to give it that touch of glamour.

40

Judy Meadows wears purple suit against background of water.

Accessories

Earrings and necklaces, if not too ornate, add to the glamorous effect. Furs also make wonderful props for head-and-shoulder portraits. If your model does not have a fur piece and cannot borrow one, make a trip to your local secondhand store or Salvation Army. They often have fur pieces that photograph well and cost only a dollar or two. My helpful wife thought of this idea one day when, in the dead of summer, we needed a fur parka for a snow close-up. She found a cleaned and sterilized white fur which cost only $2.50 and sewed it to a piece of red material. It served the purpose beautifully. Having an assistant who is constantly scouting for new and original ideas in clothing is a big help, but you can have an assistant, too. Let your model help you. Most beginners, and I can well remember how I was, are too reticent in asking a model to give some thought to what she'll wear. If she shows up in a blaze of color, sporting a print that resembles an old country garden,

The style of manufactured bathing suits has improved in the last few years as is evidenced by this bikini (left). The custom suit (right) features a low neckline and a high leg line.

This custom-made suit features a high leg line.

don't be afraid to let her know it won't do. Use tact, but convince her that a simple blouse of any solid color would be much more flattering—photographically speaking. Usually girls are more than happy to co-operate in securing the proper wardrobe. One of my first, and favorite models, Pat Hall, whose scrapbook is filled with over 25,000 pictures of herself, was constantly dreaming up new ideas for costumes. She would usually show me a scrap of material, not even hemmed, and enthusiastically brief me on what a sensational picture it would make. She was right most of the time. So it isn't necessary to have a finished costume, as long as it passes photographically.

Feature the Girl

The bathing beauty is really not difficult to clothe if the photographer keeps in mind that it is the girl he is featuring, and not the clothes. The typical pin-up model must wear a form-fitting suit. One that is cut high on the sides to give a longer leg line. The suit doesn't necessarily have to be made to swim in, as long as it fits well so that the model doesn't have to worry about adjusting it every time she changes poses or moves slightly. With the introduction of bikini-style bathing suits, many photographer's models have been making their own. Some of the photographic magazines carry advertisements on bikini suits, and even if you don't want to invest in one, your model may feel it is worthwhile for her to get it. Bikini suits are advertised in most of the women's magazines and there are several costume-like houses that

43

specialize in photographic attire. The bikini suit is only good on girls who feel comfortable in it. If your model is at all modest, don't force her to wear briefer attire than she wishes. It takes a typical outdoor girl with a tanned body to wear brief suits of any kind.

Clothespins and Such

While dresses, blouses, skirts, and even shorts can be adjusted to fit the model by using clothespins or safety pins, this doesn't work with bathing suits. Your model must feel free to pose without worry of showing tucks and pins.

One easy way to make a form-fitting suit is to purchase a yard of tubular jersey. This is sold at almost any yardage store. Sew it together in the middle of one end and you have a suit.

Sometimes it's fun to see how a model works out her own designs. I remember handing one model a piece of material which I had thrust into my old kit bag at the last minute. "Here, see what you can do with this," I challenged, as I left the beach in search of some hamburgers. When I returned, she had transformed it into a very fetching and original outfit. In fact, I sold two covers from that particular creation.

In the one-piece suit it is best to use solid colors. On the two-piece suits, checks, stripes, or dots add style and originality to the costume. But never use flowered prints. Shorts and sweater are always good pin-up material. The shorts should be briefly cut, not the long square drawers prescribed by high-fashion magazines. Capri pants and blouses, hip huggers, are also provocative costumes, and sometimes a man's shirt that hits just where a bathing suit would come is good for girls who have pretty legs.

Conservative shorty nightgown and panties serve as costume for junior miss.

A Favorite Costume

One of my favorite costumes for the girl with pretty legs and figure is a leotard and black net hose. Either outdoors or in, it gives the figure a streamlined look. There are stores that sell dancing costumes such as leotards, stockings, tap and ballet shoes exclusively. One such company is Capezio. While they may not be represented in every city, one could write either to New York or Los Angeles and they would be happy to furnish any information on their stock.

For the Tall and Thin

If your subject is tall and thin and falls into the fashion category, she can be made to look just as glamorous and attractive by sticking to fashion poses and clothes . . . not necessarily the extremely high-fashion technique, although that's fine for variety. If she wants pictures for her personal album, or to aid her in pursuing the modeling profession, they'll have a much more professional look if you keep these things in mind.

Model is framed by foliage when using backlighting on this rustic road. Indoor fashion calls for model who can "feel" the mood of the costume.

Suits, skirts, and dresses are often aided by using clothespins to tighten a waistline or narrow a hemline. Tissue paper, under a shirt or tucked into sleeves, helps to puff them out if that is the effect desired. But always see that the clothes are pressed. Every wrinkle or crease takes away from the professional look. The fashion model can achieve the glamour touch by using negligees or evening gowns, but the accent should be on the gown, and the face should be impersonal. Study the poses in the slick fashion magazines to get a better understanding of the technique used.

46

Chapter V

WHAT TO DO ABOUT MAKE-UP

A FACE with a scrubbed clean look has always held more appeal for me than one covered with make-up, even though the application has been expertly handled. My camera, however, being purely mechanical, has an entirely different reaction. It can change a thing of beauty into a nightmare without a twinge of conscience. Because of what the lens does to the face, I have been forced to learn the value of make-up. I'm speaking now primarily of close-ups or portraits, whether they be indoor or outdoor. On full-length pictures, the face occupies such a small area of the film that make-up isn't important.

A skilled make-up technician can actually change the shape of a face merely by analytical application. For the amateur or professional photographer this isn't necessary. We don't wish to change it, merely to enhance it. But there are very few girls who can be photographed without make-up. Even the most flawless skin usually appears uneven or slightly blotchy, under the camera's scrutiny. For this reason it would be worth your while to familiarize yourself with the basic steps in applying make-up.

It Saves Time

"But negatives can be retouched," you say. That's true, but retouching costs and labor can be cut in half, and sometimes entirely eliminated, by using make-up on your model. Especially if you have a small-size camera. It's almost impossible to retouch a small negative satisfactorily. Then, too, there's color film. Retouching color transparencies is a completely different technique and must be done by experts. It's expensive, too; the costs for most transparencies run from three dollars to seventy-five dollars.

Aside from the additional expense avoided by using make-up, its

Without make-up and hair styling the model (left) loses her spark, and blemishes are apparent. With eye make-up, a foundation base, and a change of hair style, our model (right) shows more sparkle. She looks like a different person.

main advantage is that it provides a much more flattering set of proofs to select from. Freckles, blemishes, lines all look more prominent on film than in reality. If you show your model a freckle-faced reproduction of herself, she'll blame you as a photographer, not her freckles.

Don't Let Her Overdo It

If your model knows how to handle make-up, so much the better. Just tell her what you want and let her apply it. But stay close by to supervise. The two main things to watch are the lipstick and eyebrow application.

Some women use a lipstick brush like a house painter. Somewhere they heard that thick lips are sexy. They are. But not when they're painted on.

Eyebrows are another feature that can go to extremes—from the John L. Lewis influence to a fine pencil line. Happy mediums are what we strive for.

48

The Ideal Face

Photographically, the oval face is the ideal shape. If you want to experiment in the more tricky features of make-up, the application of lighter or darker shades can give the illusion of changing the facial shape. If your subject has a very narrow jaw, that area should be lightened with a light shade of pancake make-up or powder. On the other hand, if the jaw is square, it should be darkened. Shadowing like this requires two shades of make-up base, a light and a dark. Unless you feel that you have a particular flare for corrective make-up, it is best to stick to the elemental steps and avoid complicated applications.

The set of pictures shown here demonstrates the step-by-step use of foundation, rouge, eyebrow pencil, eye shadow, lipstick, and mascara. Pancake-type make-up is the best over-all cover foundation. It is applied with a damp sponge which makes it easier to obtain a smooth and even surface. There are various types of pancake make-up sold at drugstores and cosmetic counters, and one cake lasts a long time. I usually buy the light tan shade rather than the pink tones. In taking color pictures, the pink tones give too reddish a cast to the skin.

Use either a cream or powder rouge, whichever you have most control over. I use a cream rouge because it can be spread easily with the fingertips. If you don't have rouge, lipstick can be substituted, but it is not as creamy as the rouge and must be dabbed on carefully in order to keep it from looking blotchy.

An eyebrow pencil and mascara can be purchased at any ten-cent store. Black is used more often than brown. The pencil should be sharpened well before using it, so that its strokes simulate the fine hairlines of the eyebrows.

Eye shadow can be bought in a small container, and it is used in such small quantities that it lasts a long time. It isn't always necessary, but does help to make the eyes appear larger. It gives them depth.

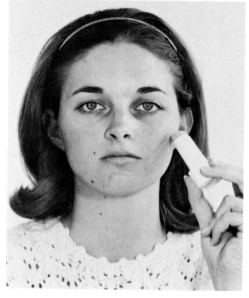 

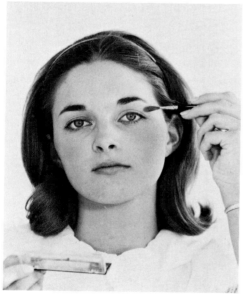 

(1) Apply pancake or pancake stick make-up to the entire face. If moles or large freckles still show, cover them with a dot of extra light make-up base.
(2) Apply cake rouge with a brush.
(3) Apply cake eye shadow with a brush.
(4) False eyelashes are not always necessary but they do enhance the eyes and sometimes eliminate the use of mascara.

50

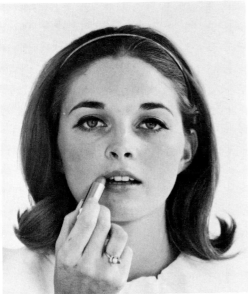 

(5) If eyebrows need shaping, use a very sharp eyebrow pencil and simulate fine hair strokes.

(6) Eye liner covers the line where the false eyelashes are applied. Even without false lashes a line carefully drawn adds depth to the eyes.

(7) Last step—very light lipstick.

(8) Finished product—a new face!

Chapter VI

BACKGROUNDS AND CAMERA ANGLES

IT'S easy enough to spot bad backgrounds in a finished negative or print, but that isn't always the photographer's first concern when he has a pretty girl in front of his lens. Whether you have a large viewfinder, ground glass, or small viewfinder, you should, whenever pos-

In fashion work the clothes should stand out against the background. In this case the bright sun in the background helps achieve this effect.

52

Edy Williams posing at the beach with sky and ocean background complementing her figure. Just a quarter turn by both model and camera would result in a cluttered background of parking area.

sible, examine the scene visually from the lens level and check the relationship of the subject to the background—*before you take any pictures!*

It should be examined from several angles, both high and low, especially if you are in surroundings that offer nothing in the way of a simple background such as plain walls, sky and sand, grass, etc.

Sometimes a Ladder Helps

On one occasion I used the street in front of my building as a background for a fashion shot. The street is paved on one side only; the other is gravel. By using a ladder and my seven-foot tripod, I was able to shoot down, eliminating the ugly telephone poles, wires, cars, and buildings that cluttered up the eye-level picture.

Not enough can be said for shooting from a new and fresh approach.

53

When photographing Edy Williams at Malibu beach, I made some tests to prove how a minute's study of background and model relationship can improve a picture. First Edy knelt in the sand, but boats and hillside were fighting for attention. We both made a quarter turn and immediately the background was improved to that of sky and sand.

The non-professional is not always able to take the time to drive to a beach, lake, or park. But that should not be used as an excuse for poor backgrounds. A lawn, a garage door, plain sky, brick walls, interesting architectural structures, all make interesting contrast for your subject.

A Trick for Eliminating Backgrounds

The lazy man's way of eliminating problems of background is to throw it out of focus. This is a technique applied to much of the high-fashion photography. It is done by shooting with the lens wide open, and at a fast shutter speed. For example, if normal exposure is 1/100th of a second at f/8, you will have to use a fast shutter of 1/500th when you open up to f/3.5. The longer the focal length of the lens, the easier it will be to throw your background out of focus. Naturally it would be more difficult with a short 50mm lens on a 35mm camera than it would be with a telephoto or long lens on a large negative.

Improper Settings

Worse than a poor background is a model placed in an improper setting. For example, the picture of a model in high heels and bathing suit posed against a car has a phony, artificial feeling. But place the same girl, in the same suit minus the shoes, in a beach atmosphere, and it immediately takes on a fresh, wholesome attitude.

Shooting with a fast shutter speed with lens wide open throws a distracting background out of focus.

This picture (left) would have been better with a clear sky as background but was saved by out-of-focus foliage. Pool water makes an attractive background for this nude subject (right).

Shoot Against the Sky

A good trick, if you have any doubts about your background, is to use sky for a background by placing your camera low. I have a small section of board fence, three feet high and eight feet wide. I keep it on my roof and have found that by placing it against the parapet, and then sprinkling sand on the roof in the area of the fence, shooting from a low angle, it is hard to detect it from an actual beach scene. I've even changed the setting to that of a farm by having the model sit down and lean against it, using a bale of hay at one side to make the scene a little more convincing.

I forgot to mention that the section of boards is not nailed. I merely stand the boards close to each other and it looks as though they are joined together. This way they are easily moved and stored.

55

The difference in high and low angle is illustrated here. Judy Meadows poses to show how a low angle lengthens.

We have a supply of bathing suits in a small dressing room. Here Penny Holland holds up one for consideration.

When shooting pictures indoors, you can use either the storytelling background, or a glamour, studio type. The natural backgrounds of dressing table, bed, couch, or individual rooms would be well used in the storytelling picture, while plain backgrounds can be improvised to suit the studio-type sitting. I know of one famous photographer who used an old army blanket for most of his portrait sittings. I've found that nine-foot-wide paper rolls make wonderful indoor backgrounds because they hide the joint where the wall meets the floor, when shooting full-length pictures. These paper rolls cost about seven dollars and can be purchased at sign-painters' supply houses. For close-ups, any piece of yardage, about a yard and a half long, especially if it has an interesting texture, helps to add glamour.

Try New Backgrounds

It's fun to use your imagination experimenting with different materials to see how they appear as backgrounds. Once I made use of the tinfoil wrappings of film packages by fastening the individual squares on a wire frame. When I shot the picture, I purposely threw the background out of focus, and the result was a diffused sparkle.

57

For close-ups, any piece of yardage, if it has an interesting texture, helps to add glamour.

Exposed stones of patio almost match the pattern of the model's bathing suit. A plain lounge chair breaks up the pattern.

Chapter VII

POSING AND COMPOSING

WE'RE all victims of the rectangle. Our pictures have to fit within that rigid, uncompromising shape, so we do many strange things to *make* them fit. Then we talk, talk, talk to explain how smart we were to do what we did. And most of it is nonsense.

The beginner hears so much talk about "composition" and is so confused by the din, the double-talk, and the technical problems, that it's no wonder he forgets all about the girl before his camera and, in utter despair, accepts almost *any* kind of picture, provided it's in fair focus and is exposed somehow within the film's amazing latitude. The miracle to him at that point is that he has captured *anything* on his film.

Two Ways to Frame Your Picture

But we do have to work within that blessed rectangle, whether it be square or oblong, so let's explore the subject a bit. There are two ways to frame the picture within that shape:

(1) by moving the frame, or viewfinder, from place to place as a landscape artist does, until the composition is pleasing, or

(2) by setting up the frame first, and then moving the component parts of the picture around until the arrangement forms a well-balanced composition within the frame.

The first method works better with scenic photograpny, while for photographing women, the second is best. Think of your model as a line, or form, framed within that rectangle. The effect of the finished picture depends on your feeling for line and space, and on your skill at arranging the various parts of the body *before* you take the picture.

61

Emphasize the model by posing her diagonally against a plain background.

A Few Pointers

Before we get to the actual posing, here are a few rules that can help you to improve your composition:

(1) Use the entire negative by composing to the edges at the time you take the picture. This may take a few seconds longer, but there is no point in sacrificing quality later by being forced to enlarge only a small portion of the whole negative area. Don't be afraid to get your camera close to the model. If the picture you want is a close shot, take it that way in the first place.

I have seen pictures of a girl standing in the middle of a large blank area of sand and sky. The total height of the figure is only about $\frac{1}{4}$ of the full negative. If it is the girl you are photographing, forget the scenery around her and let her have a chance. Of course, some finders are easier to compose with than others. Checking the ground glass is the best way to know exactly what you are getting on the final

62

I have built a mirrored stand which I place next to the camera. This is a great help in posing the model since she can see the right and wrong angles.

film. If you are considering buying a camera, this is a feature to look for. The twin-lens and single-lens reflex cameras have a ground glass . . . yet the picture can be seen up to the very moment of exposure. With this type of camera there is no reason not to compose to the edges of your negative.

(2) Try to compose your pictures with strong diagonal lines. This is very pleasing to the eye and can help bring the camera closer to your model. In a full length, the head can be near one corner and the feet near the other.

Keep These in Mind

When I first started photographing models on the beach a few years ago, it was difficult for me to explain to them just what I wanted. In fact, I'm not sure that I myself knew what I wanted. The unimaginative results I got only made me more determined to analyze the reasons for my failure to capture natural, yet flattering poses. In studying my prints later I found many of the answers . . . and discovered many ways of improving my work. Here are a few things to consider:

(1) *Use a mirror.* One of the first things I learned was that a mirror placed next to the camera makes it easier for the girl, whether experienced or not, to pose herself in a flattering manner. All women like to look in mirrors and can spot an ungraceful line a lot easier than the cameraman can. The mirror has become so vital a piece of

63

basic photo equipment for me that I have made a stand for it out of pipe and wheels, and push it behind the camera so that the subject can see herself. When shooting outdoors, I carry a smaller mirror (easier for the model to carry!).

On only one occasion can I remember having regrets about bringing a mirror along. My model happened to be the narcissus type. She used to become so completely hypnotized by her own image that I had one devil of a time getting her to look into the camera. She just couldn't take her eyes off herself. When I'd miraculously manage to get her attention for a moment, her eyes would invariably flash back to the mirror just as I clicked the shutter. I ended up by burying the mirror in the sand when she wasn't looking. And that wasn't easy, either.

Baseball diamond at a neighborhood park makes a good location for this brief costume.

The shallow surf lends itself to natural poses.
Larger image of model is possible by cropping just above the knee.

(2) *Get an experienced model.* As a beginner, I found that photographing a model who had some experience made good pictures when I myself didn't know what to tell them to do. By "experienced" I don't mean a girl who has posed for professional photographers. Even if she has only practiced posing before a mirror at home, or has had lots of snapshots taken by friends or relatives, that's enough experience. When Pat Hall first came to see me, she had nothing to show me except some snapshots taken with a box brownie . . . but the poses were so unique that I knew at once that she would make a good model. She wasn't afraid to suggest poses, and she loved the job of modeling. That's one of the reasons she became a top model.

(3) *Learn to recognize the good poses.* You and your model can get to know the good poses by studying the magazines and keeping a file of pictures that you like. Take this file with you the next time you go out to take pictures. You needn't copy the pictures exactly, but one pose usually suggests a dozen more. Don't be afraid to try ideas that appear silly. Later, they may prove to be the best ones. When collecting pictures for reference, don't let your conscience bother you. All the best photographers I know keep such a file of the work of other photographers. They call it a *morgue.* It's used to stimulate their own ideas.

I usually suggest a pose and then have the model, in this case, Susan Molina, vary it by changing it slightly (left). The head looks more comfortable and natural (right) than in the original pose.

Use plenty of film and take slight variations of each pose by moving an arm or leg a few inches at a time. Sometimes, just a small change can mean the difference between a graceful or an awkward pose.

(4) *Divide the body.* This isn't as gruesome as it sounds. The trick is to study only one part of the figure at a time. I divide the girl into four parts (only with my eyes, so it doesn't hurt): the legs, torso, arms, and head. In a full-length pose, I make sure that the legs are well posed, first. Try for a graceful line, and make sure that it is the best angle. Look for any distracting bumps or bulges. Often, if the model presses one leg against the other, it will make a bulge. Next, I make sure that the torso is turned at the correct angle, so that the hips are not "flat on" to the camera. The most flattering angle for the torso is a 3/4 or side view because it narrows the hips and accentuates the bust line.

Next, the arms should be arranged so that they do not hide the bust line, from the front or rear.

Last, worry about the head. Study the girl for her best angle. Thin faces are usually better straight on; wide faces, turned 3/4. If her nose is long, tilt her head back. If her jaw is wide, tilt her head down. If she has a wide face, long nose, and box jaw, just shoot her—with a Colt automatic.

Head is too strained (left). Natural position seated in surf (right) is the final result of this particular posing sequence.

(5) *Correct defects by angling.* Many times your model will have some slight imperfection. The idea then is to find her best feature and accentuate it.

For example, if your girl has beautiful legs, look for poses that emphasize them. Get your camera low so that most of the picture is leg. Shoot some lying-down poses with her legs up in the air. Show her climbing fences, etc.

If her torso is well formed, and her legs are thin, or too fat, pose her on her knees, with her legs curled up under her, or try some close-up shots where the legs are not shown at all. If her hips are too large, have her bend forward from the waist so that the hips are the farthest from the camera. That makes them appear much smaller.

The right costume can also do much to hide flaws in the figure. A girl with a heavy body, though beautiful face and shoulders, looks better in an off-the-shoulder dress. To look well in a bathing suit, a girl must have long, shapely legs, slim hips, a small waist and a full bust.

(6) *Use props.* The best way to get poses, I find, is by using props. They have a way of suggesting to the model what she should be doing. It is very difficult for even the most experienced model to strike an interesting pose when she has nothing to do. Props give the picture a story, a reason for being taken. Props can also be a help when you have milked your last idea. Be on the lookout for good props.

Low camera angle with model leaning forward emphasizes the bust line and gives a clear sky area behind the model.

The diagonal pose flatters and strengthens the leg line.

Either take them with you, or use the ones you find at the scene. At the beach you can usually find boats, rocks, piers, sand dunes, logs, seaweed. Each of these will suggest dozens of poses . . . climbing, standing, sitting, kneeling. Other good aids are such movable props as beach balls, hats, sunglasses, colorful towels, even swim fins. All these help make the model's job easier and more pleasant.

In the country, you can find fences, trees, haystacks, rivers, more boats, docks, and hundreds of other idea-provoking props. Even the city, with its rooftops, windows, and parks, has many props that can suggest interesting poses for you and your model to try.

(7) *Use a posing chart.* Recently, I found that it was easier to show the model a *picture* of what I wanted, than it was for me to try and twist my 6'3" frame into a pretzel pose. I made up a posing chart of some favorite poses taken of other models. The card is only about 5x7 inches and shows a couple of dozen varied poses. I find that it serves as a wonderful ice-breaker. I usually let the girl look it over at first, and then I ask her which is her favorite pose. When she has

69

Posing Chart.

Make sure that the prop does not dominate the model, but is something she can use to benefit her posing.

chosen one, and copied it, we make a slight variation, and then it becomes a new pose. The card is divided into posing groups: standing, seated, kneeling. From these, a whole new series emerges when working with a new model. You might try using such a chart by showing either your own past favorites or those of other photographers whose work you admire.

To sum up: Remember to use your full negative . . . think in terms of good composition, watch the diagonals, keep the subject away from dead center . . . hold your camera close to the model . . . try using a mirror whenever possible . . . remember that experienced models are the best to work with . . . keep a file of ideas . . . study your model's figure in sections . . . learn to hide her bad features and emphasize her good ones . . . be on the alert for good props . . . make up a posing chart. If you remember even a few of these things, you'll find a definite improvement in the quality of your pictures.

71

Chapter VIII

DAYLIGHT

DAYLIGHT is not only the most convenient photographic light source, but it is, if controlled properly, the most flattering. There has yet to be invented a light that can match the sun or duplicate the softness of indirect daylight.

This is especially advantageous to the beginner because daylight does not require a lot of equipment. Natural light is preferred by many professional photographers, and in fashion work it is used almost exclusively.

Since there are various types of daylight, it's a good idea to classify them in four categories: bright sun, cloudy sun, shade, and indoor daylight.

Correct Exposure

Deciding on the correct exposure is one of the first problems of the beginner and the last of the professional. There is an easy way to be sure of a correct exposure ninety per cent of the time. Learn three or four basic exposures, one for each kind of light, and adjust your exposures accordingly.

First, though, you must understand the principle of the *f* stops and shutter speeds.

The f *Stops*

The *f* stops determine the size of your lens opening (aperture). The smaller the number, the larger the opening, the more light. The shutter speeds determine the length of time the light affects the negative. The two must be balanced to compensate for each other, and the result is your exposure. The *f* stands for the term *factor,* which is the symbol for an arithmetical proportion: the relation between the diameter of the lens wide open (*aperture*) and the *focal length* of the lens, usually given in inches. For instance, a 2″ lens with an aperture of 1″ is rated at *f*2. On the other hand, a lens with an aperture of 1″ but a focal length of $3\frac{1}{2}$″ is rated as *f*3.5.

If you're striving for depth of field where foreground and distance are in focus, use a small aperture with slow shutter speed. This picture was made at 1/25th at f/22.

If you wish to stop action as in this picture of Lisa Hamilton, a very fast shutter speed is required with a larger opening. This was shot at 1/500th at f/5.6.

How It Works

Thus several combinations of aperture and shutter speed will allow an equal amount of light to strike the film, but with different results to the finished picture. Small openings carry greater depth of field (distant objects are as much in focus as those in foreground) but require slower shutter speeds. Faster shutter speeds stop action, but in turn require larger apertures. If you're striving for depth of field, as shown in the picture of the girl with a wheel in the foreground (where both are in sharp focus), you would use a small aperture with slow shutter speed, i.e., 1/25th f/22.

But, if you wish to stop action, as shown in the picture of the dancing girl, a much faster shutter speed would be required with a larger opening, i.e., 1/500th f/5.6. Because the wide aperture will reduce the depth of field, it is important that your focus on the moving figure be accurate. There will be very little leeway of sharpness in front of and behind the subject.

If you use an exposure meter, set the film-speed indicator to the proper film speed (provided by the film manufacturer in each package) and match the dial setting to the light reading on the meter. Be sure to read the important part of the scene (usually the face); don't accidentally tip the meter toward the sky, and don't create a shadow as you make your reading. Here again testing is important.

If you use a meter, be sure that you take a reading close enough to the subject so that you don't record the overbright sky.

I've found that a basic general exposure for most outdoor shots is 1/250th at $f/9$. The fast shutter speed will stop most action, and $f/9$ is all the depth I need. It is also about the sharpest f stop on the Rolleiflex because it is between the widest and the smallest opening.

The following chart could be used as a guide for those of you who do not have a meter:

BASIC EXPOSURE CHART
[For Medium speed film—ASA #40]

Bright Sun	Cloudy Sun	Shade	Window Light
	1/1000th f/2.5	1/250th f/2.5	1/50th f/2.5
1/1000th f/4.5	1/500th f/3.5	1/100th f/4	1/25th f/4
1/500th f/6.3	1/250th f/5	1/50th f/5.6	1/10th f/6.3
1/250th f/9	1/100th f/8	1/25th f/8	1/5th f/9
1/100th f/12.5	1/50th f/11	1/10th f/12.5	1/2 f/16
1/50th f/18	1/25th f/16	1/5th f/18	1 sec f/22
1/25th f/25	1/10th f/25	1/2 sec f/25	2 sec f/22

Exposures underlined are my particular choice because I prefer the f stop between the widest and smallest opening. My lens goes from $f/3.5$ to $f/22$ so that $f/8$ or $f/9$ is considered the sharpest with a medium depth of field. These exposures are based on Adox R-17 film developed for 8 minutes at 68 degrees in D-76.

Noon Has Its Dangers

The brightest sun is at noon—the hour when box brownies come out and cast their shadows: deep, dark shadows instead of eyes, mustache under the nose, black collar around the neck. This is the common result of most pictures taken at noon. One rule the professional learns early in his career is that sunlight directly above the subject is the poorest type of lighting. He avoids it. Better wait until later in the day, or shoot earlier in the morning. Even then, there will be definite shadows, although from a lower and more flattering angle.

Shooting with bright sun (directly overhead) as the main source of light requires either a reflector or flash to fill in the shadow areas.

Without reflector fill-in.

With reflector fill-in.

Reflectors Are Handy

Reflectors are easy and inexpensive to make. Mine is merely a discarded cupboard door onto which I have glued tinfoil. The other side I've painted white. Any piece of wood will do, the lighter weight, the better. Even heavy cardboard is okay, although it won't stand up under rough treatment the way wood will.

One advantage of a reflector over flash is that it is inexpensive. Another advantage is that the photographer can be sure of where to place his fill-in because he can see just where the reflector's rays hit the subject. With flash, he can judge only by past results.

A reflector is more cumbersome to operate, it's true, but this can be overcome by a little preparation beforehand. I have attached a metal plate to the back of my reflector so that my tripod tilt-top can be screwed to the plate. With the use of my tripod, the reflector can be locked into the correct position and that leaves me free to operate the camera. The 7-foot tripod makes it possible to bring light from a more flattering angle by tilting it high from the ground.

The female subject, especially if she is a blonde with blue eyes, has difficulty looking into a reflector. The extreme glare, if concentrated too long, causes the eyes to water and forces an unflattering squint. It is better, then, to figure out your pose and expression before experimenting with the angle of your fill-in; then tell your model to close her eyes while you decide in what position you wish to lock the reflector. If your camera is focused, with the lens stopped down and ready to go, you can have her open her eyes at the last moment. Even then, if the day is bright and clear, your model may not be able to keep her eyes open long enough to acquire a completely natural expression. In that case, backlighting may be advisable.

Against the Light

With the subject's back turned to the light, the exposure will have to be increased. You'll need to base it on the shadow area. (Refer to the Chart—exposure is the same as for cloudy sun.) Open up the lens iris

I use the portable Reflectosal square umbrellas when working with sunlight.

Here, John Papiro, lifeguard, holds surf-rider, used as a reflector, while Spring Mitchell poses for the camera.

There are many natural reflectors such as the sand, shown here reflecting on Susan Molina.

about two stops more. The background will then be overexposed. You can avoid this by using a reflector and shooting at what would have been the normal exposure. The most successful technique for back-lighting, however, is the use of flash (see chapter on flash). With that, you expose for the light background and the flash illuminates the subject, which is in shadow.

Shade Is Best

Shade is the most flattering type of lighting for outdoor portraits. The soft, evenly spread light casts delicate shadows, and it's better than the most expensive vanishing cream for eliminating wrinkles. To shoot in the shade, the lens must be opened four stops beyond normal. Or, you can shoot at a slower speed. Exposures made in shade will usually produce flat negatives. This can be compensated for in the processing, by extending the developing time somewhat (usually about 10-25%).

The open end of a porch makes an excellent setting for this sort of portrait. By hanging a white piece of material in back of your model, far enough away so that it just catches and reflects the light, her face will have a softness that is carried through to the white background. Middle-aged and matronly women respond beautifully to this treatment. The younger girls, with flawless complexions, can usually withstand the sun's scrutinizing rays; for them, shade lighting is an added compliment.

Millicent Deming pauses to read a letter. The paper acts as a natural reflector while the sun backlights the picture.

Semi-silhouette (right) by using a high angle to include sparkle of the surf. Exposure is based on the sunset—1/100th at f/22. Low angle at sunset with model in complete silhouette and reflections in wet sand (left).

Who Cares About the Weather?

Because most of my photographic work is planned in advance, I'm never sure what the weather will be like. Not even the weatherman's report, and a review of recent conditions, can give you any comforting assurance that the weather will stay good. But it doesn't really matter, I found out.

On one occasion I began working in bright sunshine and took the last few pictures in a misty drizzle, having changed f stops twice to allow for the added exposure as the skies grew more overcast. It reminded me of those photo film ads which "Guarantee equal quality, rain or shine." The pictures justified this boast. Those taken under

81

adverse conditions were even more flattering than those taken in bright sunlight.

Soft Light Is So Easy to Use

A very helpful aspect of shade lighting, or filtered sunlight, is the variety of angles possible. Under harsh lighting, the position of your subject is restricted, but with the broad diffused light of a hazy or overcast day she is well lighted in almost any pose. Shadows are delicate, and it is possible to tilt or turn her head in any direction without danger of casting severe shadows.

For full-length pictures, particularly bathing-suit or figure studies, the soft lighting is not the most advantageous. It emphasizes mass. Since you're striving to accent line in this type of subject matter, a hard light is required.

As was noted earlier, the majority of fashion photographers prefer to work with natural light. The most popular technique involves the use of skylight. It simulates the softness of shade lighting in the studio and eliminates, to a large extent, the use of any other lights. On occasion one or two floods or reflectors are used to fill in the shadows. Some studio skylights have curtains or shutters for controlling the amount and direction of the light.

The same effect can be obtained by working next to a large window. The direction of light is the only difference. Since the daylight is indirect, filling in the shadows can be done with a 150-watt flood or spot. For this kind of lighting I add six stops more than for bright sun (see Chart for exposure).

Whenever you or your subject wish to capture a delicate mood, or a will-o'-the-wisp quality, try working with skylight or window light. If you don't have a studio, remove the draperies from any large window in your home and you'll get an effect almost as good.

Moonlight Pictures by Sunlight

And speaking of moods, have you ever tried moonlight pictures on a sunny day? Sounds crazy, but it's possible with the use of filters. Just picture a girl, in a filmy dress, standing on a hillside, perhaps a tree or other interesting bit of foliage to one side. With the use of a red filter on your camera, the sunny day (provided the sky is really blue) changes and takes on the appearance of moonlight. Your model becomes a mystical somnambulist. And here a word of warning: Be

Gwen Selvage pauses under the shade of a lifeguard station. Thus the lighting is a very soft shade.

An example of an outdoor nude taken in the shade on a sunny day. Note the exquisite plasticity of the skin tones. This was taken with a Rolleiflex at f/5.6 and 1/250th.

Moonlight by sunlight.

The use of filters is illustrated here. Their main purpose is to hold back certain colors. The best filter for skin tones is yellow; it darkens the blue background. The red filter has a tendency to wash out skin tones—notice the bright red shirt looks washed out. The model is wearing a red shirt, and is holding a yellow paper roll against a blue background.

sure to apply a very dark, almost black lipstick, for the red filter is somewhat of a vampire. It drains the lips of all color. In fact, it bleaches the skin tones considerably, and for this reason I use it only for special effects. The exposure factor is about 6x (open up 3 stops).

What Filters to Use

There are many types of filters. Filters that bring out texture (like the orange or Written G), polarizing filters that cut through the glare and also darken blue skies, red filters which spectacularly blacken the sky and any green foliage, light-green filters for portraits, and numerous other filters made especially for adjusting color film to the various light sources. It is best, then, to familiarize yourself with the one most suitable for your needs. In photographing women, the light-green filter is the most used. It darkens the sky the way a yellow filter does, yet it doesn't bleach out the skin tones. I use it almost exclusively.

Just as I advocate the use of one film, the same goes for filters. While the red filter is nice to have around for special effects, it is not really as useful as the green for photographing women.

So, to summarize this chapter on daylight, I've tried to give you the benefit of my own experience and to implant, first of all, the thought that daylight is the most variable source of lighting, a source that requires the least amount of equipment. While indoor pictures require some type of artificial light, nature itself provides numerous reflectors, filters, and diffusion screens. The sand and sea can serve as reflectors, and the clouds on overcast days are invaluable for providing a filtered, diffused light. So don't be frightened by talk of flashbulbs, reflectors, filters, and diffusion screens. Learn their functions, but use nature's own before investing in any expensive equipment.

Illustrates the use of props. The net was held by my assistant but it could just as easily have been attached to a pole, fence, or log. A prop gives the model something to do and helps her become less self-conscious.

Two floods on white paper background give shadow effect to figure.

Chapter IX

FLOOD AND SPOT LIGHTING

TOO often the novice is quick to excuse poor work with the lament that he could have done better if he'd only had some good lighting equipment. *Expensive* is what he means. When the picture is printed, no one can tell how much the lights cost. It's *where* the photographer places the lights that determines how good the picture is going to be.

Bargains Are Fun

Photography has always been considered an expensive hobby. And it can be. Particularly if the beginner feels that everything must be brand new and the best of its kind. To me that's no fun. I've always enjoyed shopping around for bargains; and, when you hunt for photographic equipment, it pays to follow the camera auctions, sales, etc.

To give you a case in point, most of the pictures in my first studio

88

were made with floodlights and reflectors costing less than five dollars each, complete with stands! I wired up the sockets myself with heavy-duty cords and plugs. I very seldom use more than four lights on any picture and some of my best are made with one or two. Occasionally I use a spotlight for a portrait or nude study. At an auction I purchased a 500-watt light, complete with Fresnel lens and stand on wheels, for fifteen dollars!

If you have the light stands and sockets attached with swivel joints, these can be used both for flood and spot lighting by simply changing the bulbs. Use the 500-watt flood when you want soft lighting and use a 150-watt reflector *spot* bulb for lighting the hair and background and a 150-watt reflector *flood* for a fill-in light.

By using these reflector spots, which cost very little, you can get a spotlight effect for backlighting when you want only a small area lighted. These mushroom-shaped bulbs can also be bought in 75- and 300-watt as well as photo flood size. I prefer the 150-watt size because the light is concentrated and is bright enough for portraits.

Floods Versus Spots

As I said before, the cost or style of the light is not as important as where it is placed. Floods will do the job as well as spots, if not better. Floods are actually more flattering because they diffuse the light. Spots

89

2

bring out "character" because the light rays are direct and throw hard shadows. Sometimes I prefer the spot for a main light because I am able to control the area of light.

For glamour pictures, hard shadows lend an air of mystery. *A word of warning, though:* Unless your subject has a flawless complexion, or you have a large negative and an expert retoucher, stick to the soft lighting.

For floods I prefer the 500-watt, 3200° Kelvin over the No. 2 photo floods because they are color corrected for Tungsten color film and have an unusually long life. No. 2 photo floods last only about 6 hours.

3

90

4

What You Can Do with Only Three Lights and a Reflector

Here is a series of pictures illustrating what can be done with just three lights and a reflector.

(Illustration No. 1) Our main light or "key" determines where the shadows will be. For a key I used a 500-watt spot (about $5) and moved it about until it cast the most flattering light on the model's face. This happened to be from the direction the model was facing. With glamour portraits the placement of the key is from this direction because it gives a flattering flat light. With character lighting on men you can get away with a more unflattering hard crosslighting.

Have the spotlight high enough to throw a small shadow below the nose. If it is too high you will get into that unflattering hard crosslight again.

(Illustration No. 2) To fill in the shadow slightly I use a Reflectasol umbrella reflector on the opposite side from the key light and as close to the model as possible without getting it into the picture range. These Reflectasol reflectors reflect a very soft light since they are so large. If you do not have such a reflector, another light may be used (about 150-watt reflector flood). Keep it close to the camera so it will not throw conflicting shadows. One set of shadows on the face is enough. The ratio between key and fill light can be changed by moving either light closer or back from the subject. With reflector, spot can be turned more on the reflector and less on the subject to bring up the fill light.

91

5

(Illustration No. 3) Our third light, another 150-watt reflector spot, was used to light the hair and placed camera right, behind our model. Since most of its light was shining into the lens, a piece of black paper was clipped to the reflector with clothespins.

When I have the key light on one side I always place the hair light on the opposite side. In this case the hair light is directly behind the model's head and the key is directly into the model's face. Care should be taken not to have the reflector spot too close on very light blondes or the hair portion will be overexposed. With dark brunettes, you will need the light closer to obtain highlights.

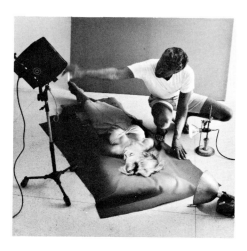 

6

(Illustration No. 4) The last light is directed to the background and can be a 500-watt flood or a 150-watt spot, depending on the amount of area you wish to cover. If you want only a small light area behind the head, use the smaller light. A flood will make the whole background light. You can compensate for this by dodging in the corners when printing. I generally have the background light on a low stand behind the model, about four or five feet from the background.

Gray Backgrounds Best for B & W

With a white background it is rather hard to get a gradation of light in the center and dark in the corners without dodging, even with a spot. A gray background, on the other hand, will turn very bright where the light strikes and fall off to black or dark gray where there are no direct rays. For this reason I prefer the gray background for black-and-white pictures.

Now for a glamour shot. Actually, there is very little difference in the two pictures except that our model has changed to an off-the-shoulder dress and we are not using a light on the background; instead, the background's 150-watt spot is directed to her bust. Crosslighting emphasizes the cleavage. This is typical of glamour shots. Cardboard can be used to keep the key light from hitting the chest and the chest light from hitting the face. Otherwise, the shadows from each light will be washed out. Remember, you are working with shadows as well as with light. The shadow, in other words, is part of the picture. Key light, fill-in light, and hair light are in the same position as for the portrait, except that they're in reverse order.

It might be a good idea to mention here that placement of the key light is usually better *above* the model than below. There are exceptions, of course, but when a key light is directed from below, it is usually for the horror-type newspaper picture. Many times, unusual effects can be obtained by experimenting with the direction of the key, but on the whole, if you want a good picture every time, and like the feeling of being sure of yourself, the key above and coming from the direction the model is looking usually is the best lighting and the safest.

For those who want to go a step further with the glamour stuff, let's try a shot with the model lying on the floor. Not only will you get a more interesting angle and picture, but the girls love it because they like the relaxed feeling of lying down. A gentle nudge now and then keeps them from dozing.

93

Now the Model's on the Floor

We put the model on the floor because our camera has to be about five feet above, and anything higher than that would make it impossible to see the ground glass without climbing. We used a couple of pillows and covered them with a square of felt. We used only three lights for this set-up: a 500-watt key, without fill, a 150-watt hair light, and a 150-watt crosslight on the bust. Simple?

The secret of this type of shot is to have your camera above the model's head so that you are shooting from above rather than below her chin. In other words, your model's feet should be pointed away from the camera. She will be upside down to your eye and right-side up on the ground glass.

Another interesting pose can be worked out by hanging the felt behind the subject, and have her roll onto her side.

To demonstrate the use of two lights, we used a nude study. Unlike the conventional portrait, the nude requires a lot more imagination in the placement of lights. To keep the demonstration graphic and simple I used two 500-watt spots and tried several variations of placement.

(Illustration No. 1) Using a hard spotlight placed to camera left with the model facing directly into the light you'll notice how the shadows are very definite and continue across the background of the floor. A picture with this type of hard light really needs retouching to soften the elbows and ribs, which are emphasized. The background goes dark because the light is concentrated on the model.

(Illustration No. 2) With the same model and same pose but substituting an umbrella light instead of the spot, we have the same shadows but they have been softened by the bounce effect of the umbrella.

1

2

3

96

4

(Illustration No. 3) The use of two spotlights and available room light. One spot is placed on either side of the model and to her rear, directed on her. These give highlights to the figure while the room light softens the shadows to some extent. If the room is completely black the same effect can be obtained by using a soft floodlight in front, or a flat reflector to bounce the light into the shadow areas.

(Illustration No. 4) Now, by placing two spotlights on the background and blacking out the room light we have a complete silhouette effect.

In summary, keep in mind that expensive equipment is not necessary . . . placement of lights is. The portrait lighting examples shown here are merely a standard used in the motion-picture studios and should not be followed slavishly. Only by experimenting can you learn what you, personally, like. Rules are meant to be broken, especially lighting rules, and some of the most distinguished photographers are those who dare to be original.

97

One light nude.

Model Venita Wolf, strobe fill with sun.

Chapter X

FLASH AND STROBE

WE HAVE discussed the use of reflectors for filling in the shadows when using bright sunlight, and the use of floods indoors with color, but those of you who are interested in more specialized equipment will want to know something about flash and strobe.

Flash and strobe are *not* the same thing. Each is a separate medium, but used for the same purpose.

Flashbulbs can be used only once and have a duration of about 1/50th second. Strobe is an electronic unit that can be used over and over and has a duration of 1/1000th to 1/5000th second.

About Strobe

Strobe has two advantages over flash: It stops action without requiring a fast shutter speed, and it eliminates the work of changing bulbs.

On the other hand, it is more costly and heavier to carry. The professional, who uses flashbulbs in large quantities, can save money in the long run by investing in a strobe unit. But for those who use flash only occasionally, it would be a luxury.

99

About Flash

In using the flash as a fill-in for black-and-white pictures outdoors, the color temperature of the flash is not important. However, when shooting color film, the color of the bulb affects the final picture. It can be easily explained this way:

White bulbs produce a yellow light in comparison to daylight, which is more of a blue. Therefore, when shooting with a white bulb, outdoors, the subject's skin tones become quite orange. To compensate for this, one should use a blue flash shield, blue flashbulbs, or dip white bulbs in that blue solution sold at any camera store.

Flashbulbs come in many sizes. But I have found through experience that the number 5 bulb is sufficient for daylight pictures.

If you prefer working with strobe, remember that its color temperature is colder than that of flash. It has just the slightest tendency to be blue, which makes it necessary to use a warming filter on the strobe light. The exact kind will depend on your film. In each package of film, a data sheet is enclosed on which is indicated just what filter, if any, will be necessary with strobe.

Test, Don't Guess!

The main difference between the professional and the amateur is that the professional establishes a certain routine of shooting. He learns certain exposures through testing and sticks to those exposures for most of his work. He cannot afford to guess. When he goes out on a job, his only concern is with the posing of the model, or the background and composition. Technical problems are nil. There is no need to keep a girl waiting in an uncomfortable position while he fools with an exposure meter or makes calculations. Testing has eliminated all these harassing details.

Too often, the manufacturers are overly enthusiastic about their product and base their high speeds on dynamite developers. This is largely responsible for much of the confusion experienced by the beginner in trying to establish a standard balance for flash.

The Exact Exposure

In just a few minutes' time, and with a small amount of film, you can arrive at the exact exposure for flash fill-in for your particular type of film, flashbulb, and development. Here is a simple system:

100

Without flash fill-in.

With flash fill-in.

(1) Set shutter speed (decide on a shutter speed you prefer). With color I use 1/25th to 1/50th because I use a tripod. With black and white I shoot at 1/250th because most of the shots are hand-held, and the faster shutter speed eliminates camera movement.

(2) Set the f stop (decide on this by using a meter or refer to exposure chart).

(3) Make first exposure with flash or strobe unit at 14'.

(4) Make second exposure with flash or strobe unit at 11'.

(5) Make third exposure with flash or strobe unit at 8'.

(6) Make fourth exposure with flash or strobe unit at 5'.

Before making each picture, place a card next to your model, with the footage printed in legible type, for reference after developments. Results may indicate that the best footage is one between two distances tested. You will be able to judge by comparing the finished prints.

Maybe all this testing sounds extravagant to you, but remember, a few sheets of film today will save you many disappointments in arriving at wrong exposures through guesswork in the future. If you do not have time to make tests before a shooting, the manufacturers provide a guide number with each package of flashbulbs. By using the guide number for the basis of your calculations, you can arrive at a fairly close exposure, but seldom a perfect one.

Guide Numbers and How to Use Them

In case you don't understand how a guide number helps, this is how it works:

In each roll, or package of film, is a data sheet which will give you your film speed number. Say, for example, the speed is 64 and you wish to use a shutter speed of 1/200th second with a #5 flashbulb. You look on the flashbulb package and find the guide number for that film is 190. Now, divide the guide number by the distance in feet from the flash to the subject. For example, the flash is 12' away from the model. Twelve divided into 190 equals 15.8. Thus your exposure would be f/16, which is the closest to 15.8 (1/200th second at f/16 with lamp 12' from subject).

Guide numbers are lowered when you use higher shutter speeds with flashbulbs (you get twice the guide number at 1/25th second as at a shutter speed of 1/500th second) because with a higher shutter

102

All four pictures were shot at the same f/stop moving the flash to different distances.

103

speed you are using only a small part of the flash. With a slow shutter, you are getting all the flash.

With strobe, on the other hand, your guide number doesn't change. You are always getting all the strobe light because your strobe is faster than your fastest shutter speed (over 1/1000th second).

Measure the Distance

Once you have standardized your exposures and footage with flash, and as an aid to keeping your distance consistent, I suggest the use of a steel rule or a piece of string attached to the bottom of your flashgun. It can be extended just before shooting the picture and put away again when not in use.

I've seldom found it necessary to use flash or strobe on indoor black-and-white pictures. The one exception is for dancing sequences. Here, again, you would have to determine your exposure and distance by testing first.

A Test for Indoor Color

In making a test for indoor color, it is advisable to set your shutter at its best synchronizing speed (around 1/25th second is best for the most sync shutters). However, be sure to use a tripod with this slow speed.

Next, determine the distance at which you want to use your flash. A guide number will give you a fairly close exposure indoors.

Now make a series of exposures on, above, and below your guide number, at intervals of half-stops. Place a cardboard in each picture, on which is written the f stop. The results will give you an exact exposure to use for future set-ups.

It's possible to get very pleasing color pictures indoors by using only two flashbulbs, but for my particular purpose (covers and calendars) I use four speedlight power units. One light is not enough because color film has less latitude than black and white and requires flatter lighting in the shadow areas.

The following would be a typical indoor color close-up:

(1) Refer to portrait lighting: 1 key light, 1 fill-in, 1 hair light, and 1 or 2 background lights.

(2) Study composition, pose, and be sure of critical focus. If you use a long focal-length lens on an extreme close-up, you'll

104

Just before taking a picture I always measure the distance of the flash or strobe.

have to allow extra exposure for bellows extension. Refer to bellows-extension chart obtainable from Eastman Kodak for a few cents.

(3) Instruct your subject to hold perfectly still while you measure the distance of the lights. I always use the fill-in light at 5 feet and the key light, hair light, and background light at 4 feet.

Since I am a professional photographer I am using the heavy-duty portable Ascor strobe units, 600 series, with three of the units having a power of 800-watt seconds and the boom light with a power of 200-watt seconds. All of these work with photo eyes, with the exception of the one connected to the shutter which triggers the rest.

On the market today are smaller strobe units, available to the beginner or serious amateur, that work on the photo-eye principle. Examples are the two Honeywell AC slave units, the 51-A and the 52-A. The 52-A is double the power of 51-A. They also have a slave unit without wires, the 60-S, which uses a 240-volt dry cell and gives 1,300 shots on a $7.00 battery.

105

Portrait lighting for indoor color.

106

M and X Sync

Most cameras now come equipped with built-in sync. Its advantages are that it requires less electrical current since it fires the bulb directly without having to energize a tripping device (or solenoid). It is excellent for strobe because it can sync up to the fastest shutter speeds and always remain constant. This built-in sync is indicated on most cameras by an "M" or an "X" setting. It is important to remember that the "M" position is used for flashbulbs only and the "X" position is used for electronic flash.

The electronic flash is instantaneous and is triggered at the exact instant the shutter is fully open, while the flashbulbs require a contact to ignite them before the shutter is fully open so that when the flashbulb reaches its peak a few milliseconds later, the bulb is fully ignited. It is apparent that if you use your "X" sync with flashbulbs, the bulb would reach its peak after the shutter is closed. If you were to use "M" sync with electronic flash the strobe would fire before the shutter is open.

Anyone using a focal plan shutter should make sure that when using electronic flash the shutter setting is on "X," because in this case when other shutter speeds are used the shutter will be only partially open, resulting in only part of a frame being exposed.

Chapter XI

ACTION ADDS IMPACT!

ACTION gives to an otherwise ordinary picture a feeling of life, of reality. The viewer has the sense that in one brief moment the photographer has captured flowing motion at the peak of perfect rhythm. Here is the feminine form displayed at its best in a beautiful dance caught for all unchanging time by the magic of photography. Now thousands can thrill to the resurrection of that split-second when form, grace, and technical perfection combined to produce an artistic masterpiece. Unquote.

The above might be the press agent's description of an action shot of a girl dancing on the beach. Sounds like quite a picture, and a large order for the photographer whose lens is not the expensive fast $f/1.5$, and his shutter doesn't go up to 1/5000th of a second. How is he going to get such thrilling action shots?

How to Stop Action at Slow Speeds

Cheer up; there are several ways to stop action with comparatively slow shutter speeds. There are ways to make a picture look like an action shot even when it isn't.

One method is posed action. This technique is especially effective with dancers. Have the model go through a few dance steps and study them carefully. When she strikes a pose that looks interesting, stop her and ask her to go into it again, this time holding it while you snap the picture. If you use this method indoors, it enables you to control the lighting, so that each area is illuminated to its best advantage. In using the posed-action method, it does not matter what camera you use, as the shutter speed isn't of prime importance. The model should be warned,

109

An example of posed action.

however, that holding as still as possible, once the action is completed to the point of shooting, will result in a sharper picture.

If you're fortunate enough to have as your model a fairly accomplished dancer who can perform leaps gracefully, you have an even better opportunity to achieve a unique action picture. By studying the leap several times to familiarize yourself with the peak of action, you are better able to judge that split-second when the action stops momentarily. The model reaches a point where she is neither going up nor down. A split-second, to be sure, but if you can be ready to fire your shutter so that it opens when that time occurs, you have a good chance of getting a good picture at 1/100th, which is a comparatively slow shutter speed. Almost every camera has a 1/100th setting, no matter how inexpensive.

110

More Tricks

Movement in the background is another device for giving the picture action when you cannot use a fast shutter speed or when you desire the effect of a blurred background with your subject sharp. This can be done in two ways: If your subject is moving, "pan" or follow the movement with your camera as you are snapping the picture. With slow shutter speeds, the effect can be very interesting. The subject suddenly acquires great speed. Try several shutter speeds and you will be able to select the best when developed.

This same idea can be used in reverse by having your subject stand still while your background moves. I rather like this effect, and use it in the ocean with a girl in the surf. She strikes an action pose and I wait for a wave to splash against her. The composition and focus are set first, and the waves gives the action. Many times I take pictures like this in color on a tripod at $1/25$th second, and if the model doesn't move the pictures are quite sharp.

Another example of moving background is that of a girl on the street with the traffic moving behind her. The amount of blur depends on the slowness of your shutter. Try some shots at $1/10$ or even $1/2$ second. You won't be able to distinguish any detail in the speeding cars, but the lack of this lends new zip to an already interesting subject. Naturally, you won't want to chance camera movement by hand-holding your camera at these slow shutter speeds, so use a tripod if you have one along. If you don't, you might try supporting your camera tightly against the nearest telephone pole.

Being action-conscious is a good idea even in your regular shooting. Using a fast shutter speed will give you much sharper pictures if you are hand-holding your camera. Though you may be as steady as the Rock of Gibraltar for most of your shots, you'll move slightly and spoil the best one unless your shutter speed can stop your body tremor.

While I prefer to shoot almost all color with the camera on a tripod, I prefer the freedom and candidness of hand-holding the camera when I use black-and-white film. For this reason I use one of the fastest shutter speeds for about every outdoor picture—$1/250$th second. I no longer say, "This looks like an action shot . . . better change my shutter." It's all ready. Shooting at $1/250$th will stop most subject action as well as any movement on my part. The f stop remains the same throughout the day, providing the sun shines . . . $f/9$. This leaves me free to pay more attention to the girl and less to the problems of exposure, which is the way I like it.

111

As for the very fast action of dancers, and of girls diving, running, or jumping, I have found that a shutter speed of 1/500th will stop them cold.

A candid figure study with water providing the action.

112

Action Indoors

Indoor action pictures are simple with the aid of flashbulbs or electronic flash. Although the regular flash lamps have a flash duration of around 1/50th second, you can use your fast shutter speeds to stop the action. Even if your camera doesn't have fast shutter speeds, you can buy the SM flashbulbs which have a shorter duration of 1/200th second. These bulbs will not only stop most peak action, but will insure you against any camera movement should you wish to hold the camera in your hands.

Many times the shadows thrown by a single flash do not produce the most pleasant lighting, so it is a good idea as a rule to use two flash-

113

bulbs. An interesting placement is to put a flash on either side of the subject for a cross-lighting effect. This gives the figure modeling and separates her from the background because of the "edge" lighting.

Another two-light set-up is one flash on the model and the other on the background. Of course you can use as many bulbs as you feel you can afford, but if you are doing a dance series, the more shots, the more bulbs, and the cost can run high both in money and in the time it takes to change them.

114

Bounce Flash

Another good lighting arrangement that saves bulbs and also gives you an all-over soft illumination is the bounce flash. Instead of aiming your flash directly at the girl, angle it to bounce off the ceiling before reaching her. Of course, the whiter and closer the ceiling, the more light you will get. Your exposure will have to be more than for direct flash, but it is easy to figure. With a white ceiling I use the guide number and open up two stops. To find the distance, measure, or guess at, the distance from flash to ceiling to subject. For example, if your flash is three feet from the ceiling and your subject is five feet from the ceiling, you add the two distances and divide the total into the flash-lamp guide number. Here, again, if you have time, a test can prove beyond a doubt what your exposure should be. To make a test, try several exposures (on, under, and over the guide number).

Strobe for Indoor Action

If you have several indoor action pictures to do, it might pay you to buy or rent a strobe. The rental cost might be less than the price of the flashbulbs you would use on a single dancing session. Strobe not only saves you money but can give you more pictures because there is no time lost in changing bulbs. Where flashbulbs go up to 1/50th second and popular between-the-lens shutters to around 1/500th second, most strobes have a flash duration of 1/5000th second. The new low-voltage strobes are fast enough to stop practically all action with a slower speed of 1/1000th second. So you can see the advantage of strobe for action.

While strobe will stop action regardless of the shutter speed indoors, the shutter speed will have to stop the action outdoors because daylight is also affecting the action. Unless a fast shutter is used with fast action, a "ghost image" will result. Here is what happens. Say, for instance, you're using strobe to fill in on an action shot, and your shutter is slow. Your main subject will be blurred because of the daylight, but the shadow area will be "stopped" because it is lighted with the strobe.

Strobe has another advantage. It can be synchronized more efficiently on shutters with built-in sync. Once the sync is in, it stays. There is no chance of its going out of adjustment, as it may with flashbulbs.

One of the fastest shutters for stopping action is the focal plane shutter. The reason for this is that narrow slit which passes over the film at a very high speed, exposing only a small area of the film at one time. With the between-the-lens shutter, the whole film is exposed at

115

Just a standing
shot.

Water adds
action.

once, between the time the shutter is opened and closed. For this reason, faster action can be stopped with the focal plane shutter than with the between-the-lens shutter, if they are both set at the same speed. Most between-the-lens shutters go up to $1/400$th and $1/500$th, while focal plane shutters go to $1/1000$th and $1/1200$th.

Keep in mind, however, that a picture with action does not necessarily require that the model or other objects actually move. Action can be implied, by the wind blowing your model's hair, by a toe pointed in the surf, by a hand poised as though waving, by a ball held overhead . . . and by many other situations that give the impression of something in motion.

116

Chapter XII

COLOR IS EASY

IN MANY ways, color is easier to shoot than black and white, especially if you are only shooting slides or transparencies and are not doing your own processing. It hardly pays the amateur, or even the professional, to process his own if he takes only a few pictures every week.

Color film is being used more each year, and there are many different processes. For this reason, the photographer who has not used much color and tries one type after another is apt to become confused at the variety of results. It is best, then, before investing time and money, to understand the basic workings of color film in general.

Watch That Light Source

One of the first things to remember in shooting color is that light sources themselves produce different colors. Daylight, for example, produces a bluish light, while flashbulbs and flood lamps have a slightly warmer, more orange color temperature.

Because it is sensitive to these different color temperatures, color film is classified into two types: daylight and Tungsten. Daylight film reproduces color correctly when used with daylight as the source of illumination. Tungsten, or indoor film, reproduces color correctly when used with a $3200°$ Kelvin light source.

It is important, then, that the illumination for color pictures be of the proper quality. For example, when shooting color film outdoors, daylight film should be used. If a flash is needed as a fill-in, the bulb should be blue to match the daylight. If a white bulb is used, the results are apt to be unbalanced, with the skin tones acquiring an orangy look. Even light reflected from nearby colored objects, such as walls,

117

How to light for color.

Flat color lighting.

rugs, grass, or brightly colored clothing, may also cause noticeable changes in the color rendering of the finished picture. Strobe lights tend to be too cold, so sometimes a warming filter is necessary over the light.

About Filters

When photographing a girl indoors, with photo floods as the light source, it may be necessary to use a warming correction filter because photo floods are slightly on the cold, blue side. I, personally, prefer to use the 500-watt floods instead. They are the same size but are color corrected to the indoor color film (3200° Kelvin). They also last much longer than the photo floods.

When using flashbulbs indoors with Tungsten color film, it is necessary to use a warming filter also because they, too, when used indoors, are "colder" or bluer than the Tungsten light.

It is possible to use daylight film indoors, and Tungsten film outdoors, but unless you are familiar with the various filters needed for proper correction, it is best to use each type of film as originally recommended.

118

Color Exposure

Exposure for color is much more critical than for black-and-white photography. That's why even the slightest variation from normal will affect the color tone of the final picture. Underexposure will darken the colors, and overexposure will lighten them. With adverse lighting conditions such as shade, overcast daylight, or indoor lighting, a good exposure meter is essential. However, in clear sun, the data sheet that comes with the film can usually be followed successfully.

Bright Days Are Best for Color

I have found that the pictures with the brightest and most perfect colors are made on clear bright days, particularly if a blue sky is desired in the finished picture. When I am doing a calendar picture outdoors where the blue sky is important, I won't even attempt the job unless the sky is bright with no haze. This does not mean that overcast days are bad—in fact some very interesting effects can be obtained by shooting color on hazy or overcast days but this is only if you are seeking the unusual. The same is true about the time of day. More perfect color is best achieved when the pictures are taken two hours after sunrise until two hours before sunset. However, some of my favorite moody pictures are those taken at sunset or early morning sunrise. At these times the pictures will retain an orange quality.

The Best Light for Color

The best placement of lighting for color, whether indoor or out, is that which reaches the subject from the direction of the camera. This front illumination helps to insure that the shadows as well as the highlights of the scene will be recorded properly.

These basic characteristics are applicable to all color film. However, there are two distinct processes of development. One is a reversal-positive process in which the film, when developed, is a positive transparency; the other produces a negative image in color from which prints are made.

Ektachrome, Ansco color, and Agfa Film are reversal-positive processes. They supply the photographer with transparencies that can be looked at through a projector or ground-glass viewing box. Prints can also be made from these transparencies by local labs if desired. Professionals prefer working with these films because they eliminate the necessity of making color prints. Engravers work better from the transparency than they do from prints.

A popular negative film is Kodacolor, which is more advantageous to the amateur who does not wish to capitalize on his photography, and who prefers prints to slides.

Although the same rules apply, as far as exposing the film is concerned, there is a little more latitude when shooting this negative process because slight variations of exposure can often be corrected in printing. With Ektachrome or Ansco color, on the other hand, the finished result is a positive which can be changed only by an expert engraver.

It isn't essential for you to be a color expert to take good color pictures. However, it is important that you understand the characteristics mentioned so that when you select a film you will be able, intelligently, to follow the suggestions given in the data sheet. As I've so often stressed, standardize your shooting technique, and you are well on your way to better pictures.

Test for Color, Too

I've found, again through testing, that for my particular equipment, a shutter speed of 1/50th second at f/8 is perfect for outdoor color using Ektachrome. For indoor color I keep the shutter at 1/25th, placing the lights always at the same distance from the subject, so that my f stop is constant. I stick to these exposures, and increase only for bellows extension or variance in emulsion. Film speeds are changing continually, as manufacturers improve them, so it's important that you always check the data sheet enclosed with each package of film.

There are many filters on the market for the color photographer; also, expensive color temperature meters, with sets of twenty or thirty filters. But if you shoot only when conditions are favorable, two or three filters are all you need. Filters change with the brand and emulsion you buy. If you are using Ansco color, you will need the specific filter they suggest in the data sheet. If you are using Eastman film, you will need the filters that *they* recommend. And you'll find that both filters are different.

Whether you plan to shoot color indoors or out, it is best to have a plan in mind, rather than to shoot with reckless abandon and then rush back to wait fearfully for the finished results.

A provocative pose was suggested by the use of this roaring-twenties costume.

Since you're investing money in color film, put a little thought behind the pictures as well and don't rely on the color alone to give you spectacular results. Give your model a couple of days' notice, so that she can be getting together some colorful costumes. If the day isn't clear and sunny (if outdoor shooting is planned), postpone the sitting until it does clear.

Start the Color Shooting with B & W!

Study the technical points of exposure, lighting, etc., so that they are clear in your mind. When all these things are coordinated, and you have arrived at some location—beach, park, pool, or even the backyard—start your sitting with black-and-white film. This gives your model a chance to relax (and you, too). It usually takes several exposures for a girl really to get into the swing of posing and to give the photographer confidence in adding his suggestions. Thus the first shots, if not too impressive, are not wasted on color. Any composition that appears to be especially pleasing can be remembered for use when the camera is loaded with color.

Above all, remember that good pictures, whether black and white or color, depend not so much on the equipment you use, but *how* you use it! Focus sharply . . . use a tripod to protect against camera movement . . . know your exposures . . . and measure your fill-in light. The rest is up to your model!

Chapter XIII

HOW TO SELL YOUR PHOTOGRAPHS

LET'S assume that you've learned how to take the picture. Now that you have it, what are you going to do with it? Showing it to friends is nice—but is that all a photograph is good for?

After all, photography can be an expensive hobby. How about making it pay off? Surely a sale now and then would not only help you financially, but would also serve as an indication of your ability.

The Secret of Making Your Hobby Pay Off

There are hundreds of markets that buy individual pictures, series of pictures, storytelling pictures. And they will buy them from you, if your material is suited to their needs. So, whether you are interested in making magazine photography your profession, or only want to sell a few pictures now and then, here are a number of helpful hints taken from my own experience. Curiously enough, I found that in listing these requirements for successful selling, the letter "S" played an important part.

STUDY MARKETS: One unusual and sometimes advantageous aspect of being a magazine photographer is that personal contact with editors and art directors is not absolutely necessary. "Whom" you know is not as important as "what" you know. And, though many magazine photographers feel that it is a *must* to visit the office of magazine editors on a regular basis, I don't go along with this belief. In the first place, an editor is usually busier than a trombone player trying to play "The Flight of the Bumble Bee" in a telephone booth. He is much more receptive to a suggestion that reaches him by mail, which he can either accept, dismiss, or put aside to consider, than he is to spending time on personal interviews. Especially with a newcomer to the field. How, then, can you know what material to submit? By studying the magazines. What better way than by looking at material already purchased.

Every magazine editor likes something different. Each magazine is slanted toward a specific buying market. The stories must be current, the pictures must be candid-looking, no flash, natural light. Photography magazines, on the other hand, will consider any type of picture, as long as it has merit. The pocket book, or sensational type of magazine,

123

buys a considerable number of individual pin-ups to space throughout the pages to encourage the "free-readers," who haunt the newsstands, to buy a copy. Then there are the sports, the women's markets, the mechanics magazines. All of these have a unique style which, if studied, will help you to know what type of pictures to shoot.

START SLOWLY: Magazine photography is not something that one can jump into overnight to make a fortune. In fact, if it's "boo-coo loot" you're after, you'd better take up a different business. There is a good living to be made in photography, and, more important, it's a pleasant way to make a living; but like anything else, one has to start slowly. Unless, of course, you have a rich relative to back you when rejection slips start rolling in. One advantage is that you can work out of your home, thus cutting down on overhead. And if you have a job that guarantees a paycheck each week, don't quit it! Work your photography in on your days off. In that way, any money made on your photographic work will be "gravy," to be invested in additional photographic equipment, or in model fees. I was fortunate when I started because I worked as an extra in the motion-picture business and sometimes worked only two days a week. Thus I could devote more time to photography.

Many people ask me if photographic schools offer much help to the beginner. My answer is always the same. If a person has the time, and can afford to go to a photographic school, he can learn a lot about techniques. But the one thing these schools don't teach you is how to sell what you take. Most of them train you to become a helper to an established photographer. This is fine, except that there aren't too many jobs of this kind available, and those there are do not pay well. The experience you get is invaluable, of course, but here, again, it depends on the individual's circumstances. There are many photographic courses offered by the State and by the Federal Government.

Photographic magazines are full of information about photographic products, techniques, markets for your pictures, etc. I learned most of my photography from reading these magazines and practicing what I read. In fact, I sold my first article to a photographic magazine. It was entitled "Glamorize Your Portraits" and I illustrated it with pictures taken in my living room with a $7.00 lens and a cheap view camera! Which proves that expensive equipment isn't really essential. It may make your work easier and faster, but to start with the picture and the idea behind it is what counts.

SPECULATE: Some photographers consider this a nasty word. But speculation is necessary for the beginner because it is the only way to let the editors know the quality of his work. But before shooting any story ideas, decide which market you are planning to submit to. In that way, you can study the format, the lighting, the angles, and so stand a better chance of selling. If it's girls you're shooting, remember that magazines buy only the most beautiful subjects. So be selective. You do not even have to go through a model agency. You can find girls through the newspapers, through TV, and by writing to magazines that carry their pictures. If a girl has not done much modeling, she may sometimes be willing to work for pictures, or on a percentage basis, because she is anxious to become known. It is easier to sell a group of pictures that make up a series than it is to sell individual shots. If you use a little brainwork and shoot a story-angle with your model, it will help to clinch a sale. Stock photos of girls in bathing suits, or with pets, or in sport clothes, are always salable, especially for commercial accounts.

Once you have established contact with an editor, through a sale of speculative work, it is more than likely that you can submit ideas for his approval before shooting other stories. He may not give you an assignment, but he will let you know whether or not he is interested. Working on assignment has advantages, but it also has disadvantages. There is a certain amount of pressure in meeting the deadline. And believe me, there's always a deadline! Then, too, there is not the amount of freedom in shooting. One is apt to try and shoot what he thinks the editor wants, and quite often miss entirely, while if he had concentrated on his own technique, it would probably have been just what the editor wanted. The only guide here is experience.

SIMPLIFY your shooting methods: There's nothing more confusing to a photographer, and to the model, than to have to fool with a lot of equipment before a picture can be taken. One of the best photographers in the country uses one camera only. No flash, no reflectors—just film and a camera. Of course, he has specialized and so he can afford to do this. But even if you don't go that far, it is best to keep your shooting as simple as possible. I use a Hasselblad for black and whites on most girl stories, taking my 4x5 Gowlandflex for color. If I'm doing an inside story, such as a nightclub or school, or wherever I must use natural lighting, I use my Pentax. I use 4 Ascors for my indoor color (heads, etc.) and a Honeywell 91-A for outdoor. When I mentioned putting money earned from photography back into equipment, this is the kind of investment I had in mind. You are thus helping to simplify your work and to speed up operations as well. Another investment that is of tremendous value is a print drier. For years I sweated over tins,

125

rolling the prints on and leaving them all night. Now with my electric drier, I can turn out 240 8x10's an hour! This might all come under the heading of—

SAVE TIME: One thing that will endear you to the heart of any magazine editor is getting out a job fast. (And *well*.) I can remember an assignment I received by wire one morning at 9:00 A.M. By midnight that night, we had shot the color, developed it, dried it, and had it in the mail. They received it the next day, special delivery, and the editor later told me he just about fell off his chair when he received it. On the black and whites, I use a roll tank that holds eight rolls at a time. Over the years I have acquired four of these, so my black-and-white developing can be handled very rapidly.

Along this same line comes standardization. By standardizing the size of film you use, your filing system, your proofing system, all your darkroom and office work will run more smoothly and quickly. We keep our file proofs on 8x10 sheets by cutting the rolls of film into three strips and proofing one roll to an 8x10 sheet of paper. The film is kept in glassine envelopes, the proofs are kept in a standard letter-file cabinet.

SPECIALIZE: An editor is like a sick person in need of a doctor. He's always looking for a specialist. It's easier to specialize, too, because your basic techniques are then more or less standardized and you know what you're doing. If there is one particular branch of photography that appeals to you more than any other, try to concentrate on that. Just because I happen to like the outdoors, the sun, the beach, doesn't mean that everyone does (though it's hard for me to understand why some people don't). There's one outstanding photographer I know who never leaves his studio. He hates the outdoors. In fact, there are hardly any windows in his place. It's big and dark and quiet. But he turns out sensational work because he likes that type of atmosphere. Other people like working with architectural subject matter. They go to pieces if the human element clutters up their ground glass. Then, there are those with winged feet. They love to travel. There are many, many magazines who buy stories on interesting out-of-the-way places. By studying the type of pictures they use and the writing that goes into their stories, it's quite possible that a bachelor, or a married man with a cooperative wife, could travel and earn a living on the stories he sells. So, whether it's girls or children, animals or scenics, try to become known for one type of photography. That doesn't mean that you do *only* that type, but it will assure you of a certain amount of assignment work because of being known in that particular field.

SCRIPT WRITING: Here is where most photographers lose out because they're either too lazy, or pull the excuse that they don't know "how" to write. Both of these are foolish because pictures that have an accompanying script (to give more continuity or story value to them) are 100% more salable than those without. Even if you just get the facts down, the editor can usually re-work these into an interesting script. When traveling, and snapping pictures of points of interest, you cannot expect to sell them if you don't get at least some caption material to go along with them. I usually carry a small tablet; and either my wife or myself writes notes on the different places that we photograph. Otherwise, it's hard to remember names and places just from the pictures.

SELLING: Selling pictures is different from selling refrigerators. You don't point out the different qualities of your work to an editor. Either he sees them or he doesn't. And whether he buys your work or rejects it depends on one thing: *whether he sees it!* One friend of mine brought over some pictures not long ago and was disgusted because he couldn't make any money out of them. "Well, have you ever sent them any place?" asked my wife. "No," he replied. And he's typical of many photographers. They want only to "take" the pictures and leave the selling to someone else. In this particular case, my wife looked at the picture, marched over to her desk, and whipped out a quick letter to one of the editors, asking our friend to sign it. She then thrust it into his hands and said, "Mail this—*now!*"

A week later he came flying into the place waving a special delivery letter. The editor wanted to buy the picture and would pay him $25.00! It was a wonderful object lesson, and according to his beginning, he should have been doing nicely by now. However, he still doesn't mail out his work—even with such encouraging results. So, if you despise typing or thinking, then get someone else to do it for you. An agent will gladly sell your black-and-white stories or pictures, but he usually takes 50%. As you see, by a little extra effort you can double your take.

STRIVE FOR ORIGINALITY: The word "originality" has caused a drastic change in photography, art, women's styles, the theatre. It seems that everything's been done before, so now the genius, the man of the hour, is the one who can turn out something different and original—no matter how crazy. In photography, this can be disastrous, especially if your results have a look-like-he's-trying-to-be-different appearance. If the picture is unusual, eye-catching, crazy, but "original," then it is more than likely to sell. This same theory applies to story techniques as well as to individual pictures. That is where the personality

127

of the photographer himself has a chance to express itself. It's not advisable to be too original on one's first assignments. By this I mean, it's better to have a "foot in the door" before startling an editor with something you thought would be original! He might have had a bad lunch and the thing might hit him the wrong way. But, by all means, look for new and different angles. An editor is always grateful to those who are willing to think up ideas, help him along with his schedules.

STOCK FILE: Once you start taking pictures on a regular basis, keep an orderly file of them. There is a lot of money to be made by selling "stock" photos. Of course, one has to gain some kind of publicity, either by putting out pamphlets or having one's work published regularly, so that commercial accounts will know how to contact you. But I've found that even today I sell pictures that were taken years ago, even before I went into business—scenics, children, animals, accident pictures. Most of the requests I get are for girls, naturally, because that is the field I've concentrated on. We consider our stockpile very valuable —like something stashed away for old age.

But in order to have it work smoothly, it's important that the pictures be kept in order, numbered, and easily available. And always get a model release on pictures that include people. If such pictures are sold for editorial purposes, a release is not always necessary, but for any kind of advertising at all, a model release is essential. I once photographed a girl at a horse show, and it was used in an advertisement no larger than a postage stamp. (I had given it to the company in exchange for some equipment.) Even though the girl's head was the size of a pin, she called me up and was ready to sue because I didn't have a release. She was right, of course, and I realized it. I consider myself lucky to have gotten off easily by making her some enlargements of the picture.

All in all, photography can become a paying hobby, or it can provide you with a fascinating avocation. But, like anything else worthwhile, it takes time, work, patience, and a sincere love of it, to get out of it everything it has to offer.